Inflation

SIMPLIFIED

What It Means to You

Inflation
SIMPLIFIED

What It Means to You

BOOKS by U.S.NEWS & WORLD REPORT
WASHINGTON, D. C.

1969

Contents

Contents

CHAPTER ONE

What Is Inflation?

Men, women and young people handle money throughout their lives, yet relatively few of them know its real value or understand how they might best preserve it. That is because few have been able to figure out what a strange ailment—called "inflation"—is doing to their money.

According to the dictionary, inflation is the state of being swollen or expanded beyond normal size. Applied to money, it means an unusual "swelling" or expansion of the supply of money relative to the supply of goods and services. The result is a rise in the prices of goods you buy.

As prices go up, the value of your money goes down. It goes down because the amount of goods and services you can buy with it goes down.

That is the essence of inflation.

For example, you now must pay $20 for a dress which cost $10 some years ago; or $100 for a woolen suit which used to sell for $50.

The dollars you use in buying this dress and this suit are worth only half as much as before. Therefore you need twice as many dollars as before to buy this same clothing.

Since people work hard for their money—and often wait long to accumulate it—they naturally resent seeing the value or the "purchasing power" of their money decline. They feel cheated. They feel cheated because they are getting less for their dollars than they had expected as their due.

They are never quite clear as to who "cheated" them—or where their missing money went. That's because the process of inflation is elusive—not as easy to grasp as a dollar bill or a coin.

Money is a physical and a tangible thing. You can see it, touch it, and hold it.

The *value* of that money (a dollar bill or a coin) is something else again. It moves up and down—in recent years, mostly down.

The very dollar bill you hold in your hand, which had a value of 100 cents some years ago, is now worth only 50 cents. And the value is not remaining at 50 cents. Next year it may be worth about 2 cents less.

So here we have a dollar bill which *physically* seems to be the same, year after year, yet is undergoing a change. One of the difficulties in understanding inflation is due to this peculiarity.

Since the piece of paper bearing the words "ONE DOLLAR" remains the same, it is widely assumed that the value of the paper and the meaning of the words will also remain unchanged. That is where the misunderstanding arises.

If our money truly reflected its changing value from month to month, or year to year, it too would be changing constantly. If the dollar bill were reduced to half its size, it might then indicate its "real" value as compared with what it was worth some years ago.

Cartoonists and artists actually do something of the kind when they illustrate the effect of inflation on the dollar. They draw a picture of a dollar which is cut in half—or they reduce the dollar to half its size.

It is not practical, of course, to keep turning out new money every month and every year to show the changing value of the dollar. Only the cartoonist gives us a physical picture demonstrating the change which is taking place.

Nevertheless, if the reader can fix firmly in his mind the fact that money is one thing and its value is another; that money may remain physically the same, but its value keeps changing constantly (for reasons to be explained later); that the real value of the dollar he holds is not the same as it was last month and probably will not be the same next month—if he can do that, he is well on the way toward understanding what inflation is all about.

You can see the impact of inflation on your dollar as you go about shopping for food, clothing, housing, transportation, medical care and all the other goods and services that you need.

As the prices keep going up and up, your dollar just does not go as far. Over a short period of time, the price increases may hardly be noticeable. But a longer period of time gives you a much better view of what's been

COST OF LIVING
(1939 equals 100)

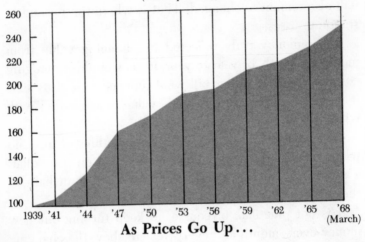

As Prices Go Up...

Source: U.S. Department of Labor

PURCHASING POWER OF THE DOLLAR
(1939 equals 100)

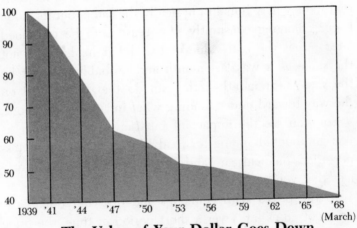

The Value of Your Dollar Goes Down

Source: U.S. Department of Labor

happening to your dollar—and you can see how it buys less bread, milk, shoes, cigarettes and movies, for example, than it did some years ago.

These figures, covering the period of 10 years, may be within the memory of many readers:

In 1958, a loaf of bread, on average, cost 19 cents. Today the same loaf costs 22 cents. Ten years ago you bought round steak for $1.04 a pound. Now the price averages $1.32. The price of a quart of milk climbed from 25 cents to 30 cents.

You could ride a bus ten years ago for a dime or 15 cents. Now you must pay 25 cents or more for the same ride.

Once it was possible to see how inflation (the falling value of money) had actually shrunk the size of a 5-cent chocolate bar. Rather than raise the price (as other manufacturers were doing), one company preferred to hold it at 5 cents and to reduce the size of the bar instead.

That was a way of raising the price of the chocolate without appearing to do so. It was a way of giving you less for your nickel—and pretending that things were pretty much the same as before.

This pretense could not be maintained indefinitely, however. As the prices of all the ingredients kept going up, the manufacturer could not solve the problem simply by reducing the size of the chocolate bar. If he had tried to do so, it would have shrunk so much as to be hardly visible at all.

Eventually, he had to admit defeat and go the way of the other producers. He raised the price to a dime—and everyone could then see that the candy had doubled in price. The nickel itself had not changed—it just would no longer buy a chocolate bar.

This recalls the disappearance of very low-priced items at Woolworth's—once known as the "Five and Dime" because nearly everything in the store sold for 5 or 10 cents. Today one has to look hard to find anything for a nickel or a dime in Woolworth's and similar chain stores.

The preceding examples indicate how the dollar buys less bread, meat, milk and bus rides as prices for these products and services increased over the past decade. If we take a longer look into the past, we see that the dollar buys even less.

A pair of shoes which cost $10 back in 1946 sells for about $25 today. Cigarettes were 17 cents 22 years ago. They are now 36 cents in many areas. Coffee has gone from 34 cents to 76 cents a pound.

The haircut which was 75 cents in 1946 is about $2 today—and the cut is no better than it was before.

If you plan to send your son or daughter to college this year, it will cost you more than twice what you would have paid the very same school had you gone there 22 years ago.

And if your plans include a new car, that will cost you about twice as much, too. The National Automobile Dealers Association estimates that the average price of a new car is $3,150—compared with the $1,640 back in 1946.

You must deliver twice as many dollars as before to buy a car or to send your children to college.

Having defined inflation, we might next consider what happens to us as individuals who have to live with it.

CHAPTER TWO

Living With Inflation

When prices rise 1 to 2 per cent a year, we have what is known as "creeping" inflation—a situation which most economists say the country as a whole can "live with" without undue hardships. A perfectly stable average price level, while much to be desired, is thought to be beyond attainment in today's world.

It's when the rate of price increases reaches 3 to 4 per cent a year, as occurred during 1967 and 1968, that we begin to encounter serious problems. When the rate gets much beyond 4 per cent, we approach what is known as "galloping" inflation. That means major trouble, especially for consumers.

In this and later chapters, we will look at some of the different ways in which inflation can affect people and also the different ways in which we can protect ourselves, or "hedge", against inflation.

We will take a look at the problems of Louis J., who has a wife and four children to support. He did not get a raise in salary this year, and he therefore must begin cutting items from his budget in order to pay the 4 per cent "inflation tax."

Marjorie J., on the other hand, got a 6 per cent raise this year, which more than compensated for the 4 per cent rise in prices.

We will also take a look at a retired couple on a fixed income, who eventually concluded that moving to another country where the cost of living is lower was the only answer for them.

Professor B. and his wife, on the other hand, because of special circumstances and their conservative manner of living, hardly feel the effects of inflation.

And Robert J. is not so much concerned with price rises as he is with the inroads made on his income by higher taxes.

John S. and his family represent another situation where inflation had a real impact. Even though John's income is steadily increasing, he has a family of growing children to support, and, therefore, his yearly expenses are also steadily increasing. Whereas under normal conditions his annual salary increases would be more than enough to take care of his family's growing needs, it is not adequate also to take care of a 4 per cent rise in prices.

These case histories, then, illustrate some of the different ways inflation can affect us. With the help of these examples as well as accompanying worksheets, you should be able to calculate fairly accurately how inflation will affect you personally, and you should be able to project your future financial situation in the event of continuing inflation.

The question that arises now is what you can do to protect yourself against the loss of buying power which results from inflation. We shall look at the relative merits of different investments, such as stocks and bonds, savings, and real estate.

For example, if you put all of your extra money into savings, on which interest accrues at the rate of, say, 4 per cent a year, you would actually lose. This is because a 4 per cent rise in prices would wipe out the amount earned as interest. In addition, you would have to pay a tax on the interest because it is income. The amount remaining would not buy as much as it would have bought a year before because the value of each dollar of savings would have gone down.

Obviously, it would not be wise, in times of inflation, to have most of your money tied up in fixed-income savings. There are, however, other investments you can make which might protect your dollars, and we will examine these later. But first, let's return for a closer look at our case histories.

No raise this year

Louis J., who was 49 years old on April 23, 1968, was born in Missouri and attended public schools in Jefferson City and Sedalia. Upon graduation from high school in 1935, he enrolled in Missouri Valley College at Marshall. The eldest of three children, he had to work his way through school, holding a night job on a local newspaper.

When Louis underwent an emergency operation for appendicitis in January of 1936, his slender cash reserves

were wiped out, and upon recovery he took a full-time
job with a newspaper at $10 a week.

Thirty-two years later, after a stint in the Army in
which he learned to speak French and German, and after
15 years in the State Department's Foreign Service, Louis
J. was back in journalism as an editor with a metropolitan
newspaper in Washington, D.C.

Along the way, he earned a bachelor of arts degree in
journalism while studying at night. In 1968, Louis's weekly
income stood at $250, just 25 times as much as he earned
on his first job in 1936.

By most standards, Louis J. achieved a moderate success in his career of journalism, despite the considerable
difficulties he encountered. With a salary of $13,000 a
year, he is well ahead of the national average for heads
of households.

During his peak years of earning, Louis J.'s father never
made over $3,000 a year—and yet he managed to live
comfortably. Of course, the demands made on this $3,000
were not as great as those made on Louis J.'s earnings.
For example, his father grew most of his own food; his
mortgage payments were only $50 a month, and he didn't
attempt to put his children through college. Taxes were
lower then, too.

As time passes, however, ways of living change, and it
would be impossible, for example, for Louis J. personally
to grow food to feed his family. Standards of living also
change. Whereas his father was content to let his children
work their own way through college if they so chose,
Louis J. feels under a certain obligation to provide higher
education for his children. And finally, prices change.

OUR SHRINKING DOLLARS
1939 to 1968

These figures show the increased amount of money you need today to make up for higher taxes and a 149 per cent increase in prices since 1939.

For example, if your income in 1939 was $5,000, you would need an income of $14,847 today to have as much purchasing power as you had then.

	Income	Fed. Income & Soc. Sec. Taxes	Buying Power Lost	Buying Power Left
1939	5,000	60	—	4,940
1968	14,847	2,527	7,380	4,940
1939	10,000	290	—	9,710
1968	31,345	7,128	14,507	9,710
1939	15,000	698	—	14,302
1968	50,754	15,085	21,367	14,302
1939	25,000	1,898	—	23,102
1968	96,669	39,053	34,514	23,102
1939	50,000	7,170	—	42,830
1968	229,771	122,953	63,988	42,830

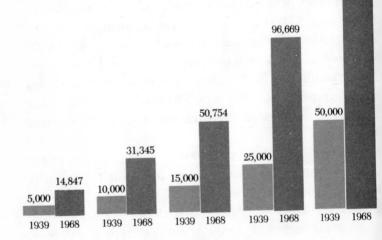

229,771

| 96,669 |
| 50,754 |
| 50,000 |
| 31,345 |
| 25,000 |
| 15,000 |
| 14,847 |
| 10,000 |
| 5,000 |

1939 1968 1939 1968 1939 1968 1939 1968 1939 1968

Based on a married couple with two children.
Source: Economic Unit, U.S. News & World Report

OUR SHRINKING DOLLARS
1946 to 1968

These figures show the increased amount of money you need today to make up for higher taxes and a 77 per cent increase in prices since 1946.

For example, if your income in 1946 was $5,000, you would need an income of $9,390 today to have as much purchasing power as you had then.

	Income	Fed. Income & Soc. Sec. Taxes	Buying Power Lost	Buying Power Left
1946	5,000	515	—	4,485
1968	9,390	1,429	3,476	4,485
1946	10,000	1,607	—	8,393
1968	18,203	3,305	6,505	8,393
1946	15,000	3,080	—	11,920
1968	26,802	5,644	9,238	11,920
1946	25,000	7,193	—	17,807
1968	43,373	11,766	13,800	17,807
1946	50,000	20,750	—	29,250
1968	83,900	31,981	22,669	29,250

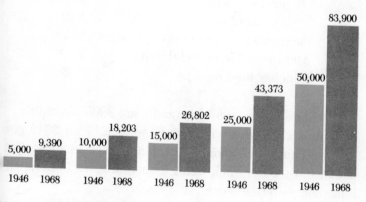

Based on a married couple with two children.
Source: Economic Unit, U.S. News & World Report

Louis J.'s monthly mortgage payments are $189 per month, compared with the $50 his father paid.

One isn't too surprised at these differences between the way Louis J. and his father lived, but what may well be surprising is how dramatically Louis J.'s manner of living can change from one year to the next purely as the direct result of one of these factors of change—price change.

If you examined Louis J.'s 1967 budget, it would look something like this:

Monthly Expenses (Louis J., his wife & 4 children)

Payments on home mortgage	$189
Groceries and milk	$200
Heat, electricity, air conditioning, water, telephone, gas	$100
Insurance	$ 50
Auto payments	$ 60
Gasoline	$ 20
Doctor bills	$ 50
Payments on tuition to two colleges	$150
Allowance for two children	$ 18
Lunches for Louis J.	$ 68

The basic expenses for his family are $905 a month.

Louis J.'s after-tax weekly income is $219—or $949 per month. Thus, each month, the family has an extra $44 which must cover such items as clothing, various repair bills, and entertainment.

Louis J. is living adequately and comfortably, if not lavishly. But right now, the outlook is for no salary increase in the near future. He already is beginning to feel the effects of rising prices, which increased at a rate of 4 per cent in 1968. It looks as if Louis J. and his family are going to have some problems.

His mortgage payments and auto payments, totaling $249 per month, are not going to change. But he can count on his other budget items increasing by at least 4 per cent. These other items total $656. A 4 per cent increase would mean another $25 a month, which has to come out of the 44 remaining dollars—leaving a monthly excess of $18. His overall expenses for the entire year are going to increase $300 because of price rises *alone*. When he has to pay increased income taxes, this will take an additional toll.

It has become increasingly clear that Louis and his wife will have to find ways to cut corners. His wife already is trying to cut down the weekly food budget by buying less expensive cuts of meat, for example.

Where else can they cut down? As it is, they rarely go to movies and their clothing budget is practically nonexistent. They can stop taking the newspaper, and perhaps cut down on gasoline by making fewer auto trips. Louis walked to work the other day—perhaps he could do it more often. But will these small economies help?

Fortunately, in a few years, the car will be paid for and the two children in college will have finished their education. But it won't be long before the other two are of college age. There seems no end to the problem.

If Louis had been given at least a 4 per cent increase in salary this year, and if he could count on a "cost of living" increase each year, he might not be able to raise his standard of living—but at least he wouldn't be going backwards.

"We may have to leave the country . . ."

The case of Louis J. leads to a consideration of a group of people who, above all others, are most vulnerable to inflation. These are retired people who have fixed incomes—pensions and Social Security. Sometimes they also get a small return from investments.

In the case of Louis J., if the family felt keenly enough about maintaining their standard of living, Louis could get a part-time job or Mrs. J. could even get a job. There are ways in which they can increase their income. But in the case of retired people, these "last resort" measures usually are not available. As prices go up, their standard of living must, of necessity, go down.

When Frank Z. retired in 1963 at the age of 65, he and his wife, Marian, had a combined income of $260 a month, including Social Security and a small annuity. It seemed quite enough.

The couple had a comfortable rental apartment in one of the Florida retirement colonies which cost them $75 a month. Marian was a careful shopper, generally managed to set an ample table for herself and her husband on $80 a month.

They also paid about $15 a month for utilities and pledged $20 to their church. They subscribed to two newspapers, held a good health insurance policy, bought the necessary drugs, and saw an occasional motion picture. Once or twice a month they dined out. Each month,

HOW INFLATION SHRINKS AN ANNUITY

This is how a monthly annuity, with which an individual or a couple may have retired in 1939, shrank to less than half its original value by 1968:

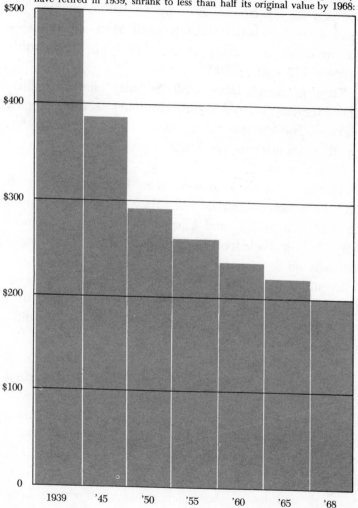

it seemed, there were a few dollars left over for savings.

By mid-1967, however, everything had changed. The rent on the apartment went up to $100 a month. The cost of food inched up slowly until Marian was forced to cut down on quality in order to keep her monthly grocery bill under $100.

True, payments from Social Security climbed a little and Medicare offered some additional security against sickness. But the general advance in prices soon blotted up their monthly reserves and forced the Z.'s to begin cutting corners.

The first things to go were their bus rides to church and the occasional movie. Then they had to cut down on their church pledge, and Marian had to search for new ways to keep their food budget reasonable. They bought virtually no new clothing.

Eventually they were forced to stop dining out completely, and even had to give up their subscription to a newspaper. Still it was becoming increasingly more difficult to break even.

What could they do?

"Frank got an idea," said Marian. "He started reading up on Mexico, about how a lot of elderly people who couldn't get by on a small retirement income in the United States had moved down there. At first it seemed like a terrible thing, getting ready to leave your country, but now we look on it as a real adventure."

Frank had heard that they could rent a nice little place there for $50 a month—which would cut their rent in half. Of course, the different language posed a problem, but he and Marian had already purchased a Spanish primer and had begun to study it in the evening.

"It's not such a difficult language," said Marian, "and I don't think Frank and I would have too much trouble. Besides, shopping in the markets is simple enough. They say the prices of most things are clearly marked and you can just point at first. It's sure to be a lot cheaper there than it is here in Florida."

Then Frank spread out a large map on the dining room table.

"You see," he said, "there's a kind of triangle formed by these three cities—Oaxaca, Pachuca and Tepic. They are all in the central plateau of Mexico. In January, you can count on temperatures of 60 degrees or so. Even in July, it's not unusual to have it no warmer than 70 degrees in the middle of the afternoon. We like that. It stays cool on the Mexican plateau because it's so high—about 5,000 feet."

Marian interrupted here. "It really could be a very good life," she said. "I might even have a servant a couple of days a week to do the washing and heavier cleaning. Another good thing would be that Frank could afford to get his hair cut oftener. You can get a haircut in Mexico for about 50 cents. When the prices went to $2.25 here, Frank just took to letting his hair grow for six weeks."

"We could get by south of the border for just about half what it's costing us to live in the United States," Frank concluded.

The bachelor girl

Marjorie J. is 23, single, a college graduate and is employed by a firm in Los Angeles as a trainee in computer programming.

After finishing college, Marjorie was eager to demonstrate her independence and strike out on her own. This goal seemed modest enough to Marjorie when she was hired at $5,980 a year. But her salary shrank about $1,150 when deductions were made for federal and state income taxes, and for Social Security and hospitalization. On each weekly payday, then, she drew $93.

Marjorie had had only limited first-hand experience with inflation until she began making the rounds to find a suitable apartment. Several months earlier, a friend had told her of a three-room apartment near her office which might become vacant. The people renting the apartment were paying $90 a month. Marjorie's father had a rule-of-thumb principle which he applied to housing costs.

"If you can rent or make your mortgage payment out of a single week's pay," said her father, "you'll come out all right."

There was just one hitch. By the time Marjorie actually applied to rent the apartment, the monthly rental was raised to $104.50.

"It's inflation," the landlord explained. "My costs have gone up, too. So I have to pass them on whenever a lease expires. Everybody in the building who extended a lease in the last year or so has had to pay more rent."

Marjorie accepted this with good grace. Her parents helped her get together some furniture, cooking utensils, dishes and bedding. Then she moved into her new home.

Budgeting her income was something new for Marjorie, too. She found that her electric bill ran about $4 a month. The telephone service for local calls was $6.50. She spent approximately $1 a day for lunches.

Preparing her own meals was exciting for Marjorie. After her initial expenditures for staples, she found she could eat quite well on a weekly budget of $15.

Like many single girls, Marjorie felt she had to have an automobile. Her parents made the down payment on a late-model convertible and she met the monthly installments of $73. Gasoline cost her at least $20 a month. The car insurance was about $15 a month. Her daily newspaper ran to $3 a month. So did the payments on her home owner's-type insurance policy. And she smoked $10 worth of cigarettes a month.

When Marjorie added up the total, she found her fixed costs for housing, food and transportation came to about $315, leaving her about $75 a month in take-home pay for savings, clothing, doctor and dentist bills, entertainment, and unforseen expenses.

Marjorie realized that she couldn't, on this budget, buy a new dress every week or go out every night, but she could live comfortably and independently, and if she spent her money wisely, she could even save up enough to go away on a short vacation.

But, again, within a few months, Marjorie noticed that she wasn't able to maintain this budget. The place where she first began to notice some change was in the price of various food items, including her lunches. At just about this time, however, Marjorie got a $360 raise, which represented a 6 per cent increase. Even after deductions for taxes and Social Security of about $72, she was making $288 more per year, or $24 per month. Assuming an over-all price increase of 4 per cent, her monthly expenditures would increase by $16, which would still leave her with $8 more per month than she had been making.

Marjorie is hardly in a desperate position. There are many ways in which she can cut down on her budget. She could, for example, share her apartment with another girl, or even, if necessary, give up her car. But if she continues to get raises regularly at a percentage greater than the rate of increase in her cost of living, she will ultimately, though narrowly, come out ahead.

No margin for error

There are situations, however, where things can be-come desperate, even when pay raises offset the steady increases in the cost of living.

Take the case of John S., who was 40 years old on March 1, 1968. He holds a white-collar job in a Detroit factory. He has a wife and five children and an annual income of slightly more than $8,000.

The oldest of the five children is aged 7. This means, of course, that John's wife, Susan, has a fulltime job at home and is not in any position to increase the family's income.

John and Susan are keenly aware that the prices of everything they buy are going up. Ten years ago, when they were first married, John's income was less than $5,000 a year. They both feel he has made good progress on the job. But the arrival of children and the increase in the cost of living in 10 years have virtually wiped out the steady gains in John's weekly paychecks.

This family has learned to accept the fact that it must live with practically nothing in reserve. In John's battered savings account, there is a balance of less than $200.

For John and Susan and their five children, existence has become a hand-to-mouth proposition. Rent, utilities and food take an alarmingly big portion of John's monthly take-home pay.

Each month, too, there are payments on the car, the washing machine and the refrigerator.

"What it boils down to," says John S., "is a case of just trying to pay our bills and keep our credit rating sound. As long as we've got that, Susan and I feel that we can take care of any emergency that might come up."

Susan had this to say:

"It's really the little things that add up—things you wouldn't think would be all that important. Like when the children want to go to the neighborhood movie. Even that costs $5 or $6. And shoes. That's the worst part. These kids go through a pair of shoes in no time. And you can't hand them down. There's really nothing left of a pair of shoes after several months of wear. I watch for the sales and sometimes I buy a dozen pair at a time. Even then, shoes cost 10 or 15 per cent more than they did a few years ago."

John and Susan presently live in one side of a rental duplex for which they pay $150 a month. Susan tries to feed the family on $40 a week, but can't always stay within that figure.

"As it is,". she says, "it's pretty much a diet of hamburger, chicken, macaroni, corn flakes, some fruit and a few vegetables. We manage a turkey on the holidays. But I honestly can't remember when I last bought any steak. Meat prices are just out of sight."

The family has a 1967 station wagon which was purchased new. There are still a half-dozen payments of $60 a month remaining.

"We hope to see a little daylight once the car is paid for," says Susan. John points out, however, that the time is fast approaching when repair bills will become an item. A new car of comparable value will eventually cost John considerably more than the one he now drives.

"It just looks like there is some kind of a high-level plot to use up my paycheck almost before I can get my hands on it," says John.

Neither Susan nor John tried to keep a family budget. "No point in it," says John. "Everything we take in, that's about $580 a month, goes right back out. What's the point in putting down, say, 'ten dollars for entertainment?' One of the kids gets sick and there's eight bucks for the doctor and five more for cough medicine and that's the way your 'entertainment' goes."

John still carries his $10,000 life-insurance policy as a war veteran. It's all he can afford, although he is keenly aware that the protection it gives Susan and the children is inadequate.

Fortunately for John and Susan, their children have had no serious medical problems. John's company provides an excellent health-insurance policy for the family. Still, the one major worry for this couple is that they may one day be confronted with a big medical bill.

"We'd just have to borrow it somewhere," says John. "That's why we put so much store in paying our bills and keeping our credit sound."

Like many another breadwinner in a similar position, John S. wants to buy a house. He's looking for one that he can get with little or no down payment and monthly installments of less than his present $150-a-month rent.

"If I could swing that," John muses, "it would give us a real lift. What we need is a place we could buy for around $12,000. That way the payments over 20 years would be about $90 a month. It's almost impossible to find something like that around here. We need four bedrooms, you know. But once in a while some old place comes on the market, maybe a little rundown. I'd be willing to fix it up on my own on the week-ends."

John and Susan both realize that home ownership could help them greatly in their struggle against inflation. On weekends, they pack the children into the station wagon, take along the Sunday classified advertisements and go house hunting. Thus far, they have been unable to find enough house for the price they can afford. But they will keep looking. They need desperately to acquire a piece of property which will rise in value over the years, as the value of their dollars goes down.

John's economic plight is intensified by inflation.

The family is in dire straits because it grew more rapidly than did the earning capacity of the breadwinner. If John and his wife were supporting only two children instead of five, they could have saved on housing, food, clothing and all the basic necessities. In that case, the problem of survival on $8,000 a year would have been much simpler.

In a sense, John and his family are suffering because he was either unwilling or unable to market his labor in a field which offered him greater opportunity for advancement. Thus, the expense of rearing a large family proved so great that John's pay increases—even though they outran by far the annual rate of inflation—were inadequate.

Inflation is hurting John and his family, however, just as it always hurts those who are least able to cope with rising prices. John and his wife cannot cope because every cent of his wages is committed before he even opens his pay envelope.

John himself doesn't place emphasis on inflation as one of this family's principal problems. He sums up his position in these words:

"We aren't complaining. Our life isn't bad, you know. It's just that we don't have any margin for error at all. I'm pretty good at my job and I'll keep on getting raises, I guess. But the way things are going, it looks to me like I'll never get more than enough money just to break even."

The bachelor

There is another group of people who are affected not so much by rises in prices as by rises in taxes.

Robert J. is a 50-year-old bachelor, a stockbroker in St. Louis, who earns $17,000 a year. Six years ago, taxes took only about one fourth of his gross income. This year they will take a full one third, leaving him with a disposable income of $11,000—a considerable drop from $17,000.

Robert concedes that he is lucky because, in the main, his capacity to earn increases faster than the cost of living. But it's clear that effects of inflation on taxes—federal, state and local—have made him aware that he's working in large measure just to support the functions of government.

Robert has done the obvious things to protect himself against the upward movements of prices. A few years ago, he bought a co-operative apartment in one of the suburban high-rise buildings. That gave him a big tax deduction for interest on his mortgage. It also assured him that his monthly payments for housing would not go up—as they might were he simply paying rent.

Still, inflation eats away at Robert's income in little ways. First, various costs at the apartment inched higher. The cost of heating it in winter and cooling it in summer went up. When he first moved in, he paid $3 a month to park his car in an allocated space near the apartment entrance. Now he pays $7 for the same privilege, and he anticipates an even further increase.

But, he says, "Where I really feel the pinch is in entertainment. If you take a girl out to dinner, you can count on dropping $20. Even movies are expensive at $2.50 or $3. In my position, where I often have to entertain groups of people, it's helpful to join a country club. But not only has the cost of food and drinks been going up; the monthly dues have been steadily increasing.

"It's difficult for a single man to get along without an automobile. If you trade every three or four years, there is always a car payment—and either you keep trading or you get nibbled to death with rising maintenance costs."

It was when his state taxes went up again, however, that Robert decided that he was going to have to cut back somewhere. The first thing he did was to drop out of the country club, which was costing him about $100 a month for dues, drinks, tips and parties. He has begun entertaining at home, which he finds he can do much more reasonably. And he now plays golf on a public course, where the greens fee is only $2.50.

"I'm not really hurting, you understand. Plenty of people are worse off than I am. I know I've got a good income by American standards. I'm right up there in the top 5 or 6 per cent in the earning bracket. But you can see from what I've told you about the way I live that $17,000 a year is a whole lot less than you might think it is when you start trying to do the things you think you ought to be able to do with that kind of income."

Making out on $12,000 a year

Some people are relatively untouched by inflation. Professor Howard B. teaches history at a small college in the Middle West. He was 50 on June 1, 1968, as was his wife, Jane. The B.'s were so impressed 25 years ago when they found that they had a common birthday that it proved the first of a series of mutual attractions. When June 1, 1943, rolled around, Howard B. married Jane.

The B.'s are a couple for whom life seems to have been especially accommodating. Howard made good marks in college, as did Jane. After their marriage, he served a two-year hitch in the Army, then got a job teaching in an

Illinois high school near Chicago. The B.'s always seemed to have an adequate income. Neither had expensive tastes, but they were not conscious of having denied themselves anything they really wanted.

Howard and Jane had two children, a son and a daughter. In the early 1950's, Howard got a master's degree in history and with it an assistant professorship at a small Illinois college. Plugging away at his studies, Howard finally got his doctorate in 1959, and with it came an increase in pay which put his annual income for the first time in five figures.

When the two children were ready for higher education, they chose to take advantage of the free tuition which was "a fringe benefit" for the children of professors at Howard's college. Thus, the B.'s avoided the crushing costs so many families face when two or more children go away to college at the same time.

Howard has always been handy around the house. He likes to pick up old pieces of furniture, work them over, and reclaim them for use in the family home. Over the years, then, the B.'s had to invest relatively little in furniture. Howard also enjoys doing various maintenance jobs around the house, which saves quite a bit on repair bills.

Jane is equally adroit in cutting corners. When the B.'s decided they ought to have an automatic washer to solve the diaper problem, Jane found one at a discount house for half price. It was marked down because it was dented. She paid cash for it.

"That washer is running just fine today," says Jane. "Who cares about a couple of dents?"

The B.'s learned, early in their marriage, that they could save a lot of money with a home freezer. It was a case of watching for food sales, buying in large lots, and then living off the stockpile. Neither Howard nor Jane can calculate exactly how much food they have on hand in their basement. But they rarely have to buy anything unless it is a real bargain. As a result, in 1967, with her husband and both her grown children to feed, Jane's food bill averaged out to $90 a month.

Because they live frugally, the B.'s have been able to buy a $100 U.S. savings bond each month for a good number of years. That's one place where the B.'s will feel the inflation pinch. Dollars put into savings bonds years ago will buy considerably less when they mature than they did when the bonds were purchased.

They always seem to have cash on hand for the occasional emergency and even a yearly vacation. In fact, just last year, Howard and Jane were able to take a 21-day tourist excursion to Europe.

The B.'s have two automobiles, a 1964 Chrysler and a 1965 Volkswagen. Both are paid for. They could easily afford newer models, but they are satisfied with the ones they have.

The mortgage on their home has only three years to run—at 4½ per cent interest.

Howard hasn't bought a new suit since 1963. "I have several sets of tweeds which I rotate," he says, "and a professor doesn't need much more than that."

Jane explains it this way:

"I suppose we lead a simple life, by most standards.

But we have our books, a cocktail or two before dinner, our friends, and just about everything we need."

What has inflation done to the B.'s?

"Not much," says Howard. "Of course, we see prices going up. But look at the way we live. We don't buy much. If you aren't out there bidding the prices up, if you don't really need too much, inflation isn't going to ruin you."

Getting ahead of inflation

Some people actually manage to get ahead in times of inflation. Generally, these are the people who know how to invest their money wisely and to create additional income through these investments. To see how this can happen, let's consider the case of Theodore Z. and his family.

For the past 12 years, Ted has been a stock broker in New York City. In 1967, his income from his work came to $36,712. His total income for the year, however, was much more. He earned additional amounts from such sources as dividends on stock, capital gains, interest and rent, bringing his total income for the year to $46,972. After paying all of his taxes—property, city, state and federal—Ted's net income was roughly $33,200.

It is apparent from the way the Z.'s live that they have improved their circumstances in recent years. Two years ago, they moved from their city apartment into a $75,000 house in Scarsdale. Their two children still attend private schools, the family now belongs to the local country club, and they have bought a second car. How did they manage all this in a decade when prices have been consistently going up and when so many other people, as we have seen, have had to lower their standard of living?

Let's have a look at Ted's income five years earlier. In 1962, his net income from all sources was $25,000. To offset 10 per cent inflation over five years, he would have had to earn at least $27,500 net in 1967 just to maintain his 1962 standard of living. But as we have seen, his net income for 1967 was, in fact, $33,200—almost $6,000 more than the minimum he needed.

Being a stockbroker, Ted knew how to invest in stocks. In 1967 alone he earned over $2,000 in dividends and more than $5,000 in capital gains. In addition, when the Z.'s moved out of the city, they didn't sell their apartment, but rented it, realizing almost $2,000 a year in rental income. They also received more than $600 in interest on their savings.

It is clear from this illustration, then, that investments in such things as stocks and real estate provide some protection in times of inflation. We will deal with such inflation "hedges" in a later chapter.

CHAPTER THREE

What You Are Worth — Minus Inflation

What are you really worth? Have you ever tried to figure out the real value of what you own and what you earn after removing the element of inflation from the total? This chapter will help you to determine the figure for yourself.

First, let's set the stage. In 1966 and 1967, the cost of living increased a total of about 6 per cent. In 1968 it went up another 4 per cent. In short, a 10 per cent rise in the cost of the necessities of life occurred over the three-year period.

How did you fare during this period of inflation? The answer is tied to two factors: your position in relative earning ability among the nation's breadwinners; and the rate at which you improved that position during the period 1966-1968.

Obviously, if your income advanced 20 per cent in a three-year period in which the cost of living rose 10 per cent, you were not one of the chief victims of inflation.

You could be suffering, of course, if your income was too low to begin with. But if you are somewhere around the national average in earning power and if you scored a 20 per cent increase over the three years in question, your position must be regarded as relatively good.

Let us first compare your annual income with the national averages for 1967. If your combined family income is $8,017, you are right on the median—which means that half the families in America earn more than you, while the other half earn less.

If you earn $10,000 or more, you are in the upper third of American families so far as annual income is concerned. About 34 per cent, or 17.3 million families, now stand at the $10,000 figure, or above.

If your family income exceeds $15,000, you are in the top 12 per cent in total earnings.

The accompanying graph helps you locate yourself on the income scale. It shows the range in earning power for all the families in the nation.

One factor not reflected in the graph is the considerable differences between the earnings of white and non-white families. The average annual income of the nation's 5 million non-white families is $5,177, which is $2,840 below the national median.

Whatever your income category, the important factor, as mentioned, is to increase your earnings each year at least by an amount equal to the rate of inflation. This is essential to uphold the purchasing power of current income and to make possible savings for the creation and building of an estate. We shall consider the impact of inflation on a person's estate in a moment.

FAMILIES BY INCOME LEVEL, 1967

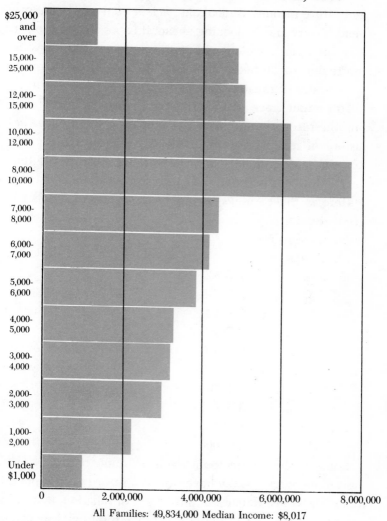

All Families: 49,834,000 Median Income: $8,017

Source: Census Bureau, U.S. Department of Commerce

First, let us see the effect of inflation on your current and future income. By looking back at your early employment history and by looking ahead, it is possible to project a set of figures which will give you some idea of your future net worth, taking into account current and possible future rates of inflation.

You might trace your past record and you might outline the record lying ahead by comparing them with the history of a representative college graduate. He is now 32 years old, and he has been working steadily for ten years. How has he fared over the past decade?

Here is the earnings record of this particular college graduate:

Annual earnings

at age	
23	$ 6,200
24	$ 7,000
25	$ 7,400
26	$ 7,900
27	$ 8,400
28	$ 8,900
29	$ 9,400
30	$ 9,900
31	$10,400
32	$11,000

Some of his contemporaries have done better. Some have done worse. Many have run up a record pretty much the same as his. Regarded in the light of inflation, it is not a bad record at all. If yours is comparable to it, you may draw these conclusions:

First, you increased your earning capacity by 77 per

cent in ten years, and each year your earnings kept well ahead of the annual rate of inflation. You thereby not only protected the purchasing power of your earned income; you also increased your earnings sufficiently so that you were able to raise your standard of living and perhaps also set aside some savings to be put into an investment of one kind or another.

The pattern of your wage increases shows that your employer, by adding $1,600 to your paycheck in the past three years, regards you as a valuable member of his team. The record suggests that you are likely to continue going up the income scale.

In trying to anticipate the future, you might continue to draw an analogy with the outlook for the young man whose record we just traced.

Let's follow him all the way to retirement at age 62. The record, divided into five-year segments of time, may show something like this:

Annual earnings

at age		
32	(1968)	$11,000
37		$15,000
42		$18,500
47		$22,500
52		$26,000
57		$30,000
62	(1998)	$35,000

With these earnings, will he be able to keep ahead of inflation? And will he be able to improve his living standard and set aside something for the future?

The answers to these questions—vital to everyone in the country—depend on the future rate of inflation. If inflation should continue to run at a pace of 4 per cent a year, it would destroy all of the increase in his earnings between 1968 and the year 2000. If your earnings should prove to be comparable to those of our college graduate, this rate of inflation obviously would have the same destructive effect on *your* future income.

This provides a dramatic illustration of the crucial impact which the national rate of inflation has on the future income of every citizen of the United States. Even if each of us should triple our annual earnings over the next 30 years—which is what our friend succeeded in doing—this still will not be enough to withstand the corrosive effect of 4 per cent inflation. Thus, what appears today to be satisfactory future progress (tripling one's income) could turn out to be an economic setback caused by factors beyond one's control—a high rate of national inflation.

The economic welfare of each citizen consequently is tied to the nation's success—or failure—in dealing with a high rate of inflation. Only if the Nixon Administration—and subsequent Governments—manage to bring and to hold the annual rate of inflation below the level of 4 per cent will we be able to reap the benefits of what appear to be respectable annual increases in earnings.

Having considered earnings, we might next turn to the effect of inflation on the value of your estate. To estimate the impact, it may be useful to draw up a balance sheet of your assets and liabilities. The accompanying sheet will help you reach the key figure in the exercise—net worth in today's dollars.

YOUR BALANCE SHEET

Assets
(The Things you own)

Liabilities
(Your debts)

Value of your home
on today's market . . . _____

Your existing
home mortgage . . . . _____

Other real estate . . . . _____

Other mortgages . . . _____

Present cash value of
your life insurance . . . _____

Installment debt on
appliances or home
furnishings . . . . . . _____

Balance in your
checking account . . . . _____

Value of your car,
or your current
equity in it . . . . _____

Remaining payments
on car . . . . _____

Your equity in pension
funds or annuities . . . _____

Your savings account . _____

Other debts . . . . . . _____

Building and Loan
account . . . . _____

Business or other assets _____

Stocks and bonds . . . . _____

Money owed to you . . _____

Total assets . . . _____

Total liabilities . . _____

Your "net worth" is the amount by which your assets exceed your liabilities. It will vary from year to year, depending on the rate of inflation, on the different kinds of investments and properties which compose your estate and on the new values, such as savings, which you add to your estate.

Certain kinds of investments, as we shall soon see, manage to ride the wave of inflation better than others. To preserve or to increase the purchasing power of an estate, one's "net worth" must increase to an extent which will equal or exceed the annual rate of inflation. To do that, it is obviously wise to keep your assets under constant review to determine which investments are meeting the challenge of inflation and which are not. Some people draw up a balance sheet of assets and liabilities each year so as to secure a fresh picture of their "net worth" in the light of inflation and general investment considerations.

We might now consider the composition of an estate in more detail.

Savings and investments

Everybody needs some savings which will grow in value, and which, at the same time, provide a reserve fund for emergencies. Those savings, assuming that they earn 4 per cent interest, just about enable you to break even—because the value of your dollar in 1968 is going down at very nearly the same rate—4 per cent a year.

So it is agreed that a savings account offers scant protection against inflation. You are going to need something more to stay afloat.

If you have a growing family, a prime necessity is

insurance. Your wife and children need to be protected in the event of your death. Insurance may be necessary for such an untimely contingency, but as an investment it leaves something to be desired. To be sure, a regular life policy will increase in value if you allow your dividends to accumulate (instead of using them to reduce the amount you must pay as your annual premium), but the eventual payment to your family will come in a fixed amount of dollars. When prices go up, the number of dollars in your insurance policy remains the same. Inflation eats away at insurance, just as it gobbles up savings.

What about your pension plan? It may look good now. Again, though, it is based on fixed amounts pegged to your earnings. True, when you earn more, your pension fund expands. But in the end, you come out with a certain number of dollars each month. Those dollars probably will not hold the value you expect and therefore will not bring you the security you want if inflation continues unchecked.

That brings us to your building and loan account. This is a good, safe form of investment and it generally offers a bit more interest than a savings account in a bank. But here, too, the rate of return is not enough to give you sufficient protection.

On the growth side, you need to have some dollars that will be working for you around the clock—dollars that will multiply fast enough to offset the losses caused by inflation.

To find out where you stand, use the worksheet on page 48. List all your savings and investments, dividing them into two parts. The first would include assets that

INVENTORY OF ASSETS

Basic Protection	Assets Likely to Grow
Savings Account . _____	Stocks . . . . _____
Building and Loan _____	Your home (estimated value 10 years from now) . . . . _____
Life Insurance . . _____	Lots, or other real estate (value in 10 years) . . . . . . _____
Bonds . . . . _____	
Your Pension Fund _____	Your business (potential value) . . _____
Other Assets . . . _____	Antiques & Paintings . . . . _____

grow slowly. The second would be made up of investments which hopefully will rise in value.

Obviously, there should be a wise division of these assets. Many people feel they should put half their investment eggs in the basket which offers basic protection and slow growth. That leaves the other half for less secure but more promising investment. There are no hard and fast rules. Fill out the worksheet and use your own judgment as to the division of your investments.

If you want to see how the dollar value of your life insurance has shrunk over the years, use the table on the next page.

In the first and second columns, write down the year in which you purchased your policy and its face value. In the third column, enter the per cent loss from inflation

WHAT YOUR LIFE INSURANCE POLICY IS WORTH TODAY

Year Taken Out	Face Value of Policy	Percent Inflation Loss	Dollar Inflation Loss	Buying Power of Policy Today

Note: If you took your policy out in 1938, subtract 60 per cent of its face value to allow for loss of purchasing power due to inflation. If you became insured in 1942, subtract 52 per cent; in 1945, 48 per cent; in 1950, 30 per cent; in 1956, 21 per cent. Interpolate for the years in between.

as indicated in the note below. In the fourth column, enter the amount of dollars represented by this loss. Subtract this amount from the face value, and enter the remainder in the last column. This final figure represents the buying power of your policy today.

For example, a $5,000 policy taken out in 1938—about 30 years ago—will have shrunk so that now it's worth only about 41 per cent as much in buying power.

Taxes figure in the inflation picture, too. To get an idea of what you will be faced with in the future, you have only to look back at what happened in the last ten years.

Take our young friend. On his first job, when he earned $6,200 a year, he paid about $885 in income taxes. In 1968, with an income of $11,000, his federal taxes went up to $1,650. If he is earning $22,500 in 1983, it is likely that his federal taxes will hit $3,500 or more. (These figures apply to a married man with no children.)

What inflation does to him in that period is something else again. For this young man, some prudent investments appear to be essential.

If your Federal and State income tax returns are handy, it may be useful to check back and see the exact trend of taxes in your specific case. The trend which you observe by looking back over the past few years will give you some idea of what to expect in the years ahead.

Whatever your position, the chances are that your taxes have been climbing steadily in recent years. It is also likely that the upward trend will continue. How much higher your taxes will go will depend on various factors: the international situation, the needs of Federal, State and local Governments for extraordinary revenue, your earnings and your investments.

If the outlook is for rising taxes and continuing inflation, in one degree or another, then the inevitable conclusion is that increasing income will be necessary in the years ahead to meet these demands on our pockets. Let's turn, now, to ideas you might consider for raising your income and protecting your savings in an attempt to keep ahead of inflation.

CHAPTER FOUR

How To Protect Yourself Against Inflation

Everyone agrees that Americans are living in a period of continuing inflation. It seems likely that prices are destined to go up and up over the long haul, though there may well be periods of relative price stability.

Naturally, the average citizen is concerned. Out of that concern come these questions—

How can I protect myself against inflation?

How can I safeguard my income and savings in a period when the value of the dollar is going down?

Let's begin with a checklist—the very basic things to keep in mind in working out your personal plan for protection against inflation.

Your Job—The record shows that a steady job is the best defense against a decline in the dollar's buying power. Wage earners and salaried people—for the last twenty years—actually have improved their lot in the face of inflation. That is because their pay rose more rapidly than prices increased.

Your Health—We don't often think of it as a defense against inflation, but good health is an important weapon in the fight. The man who is able to stay on the job steadily has generally found his income running ahead of the cost of living. The man who has been thrown out of work by illness suffers a double handicap—from loss of income and from rising prices.

Home Ownership—Owning a home has, in most instances, proved to be a worthwhile investment in a period of rising prices. People who bought homes some years ago have found, by and large, that the value of their homes has risen more than enough to offset the decline in the dollar's value. The reason for the rise is that, as labor costs and land costs go up, the replacement cost of building a house has risen—pulling up the value of existing homes. At the same time, the homeowner was favored by the Internal Revenue Service because, in making out his annual income tax return, he was allowed to deduct the full amount of the interest on his mortgage—and local property taxes, as well.

A Business—Owning a small business enterprise often can be a valuable form of protection against the effect of inflation. The assets of business tend to increase in dollar value as the general price level goes up.

Real Estate—Investing in well-located property can offer protection against inflation. Over the years, prices of houses, lots and farms have risen as the value of the dollar has dropped. A buyer must proceed with caution, however, in selecting real estate. Expert advice is called for. Not all property has advanced in value with the passing years.

Farm Property—Farms, for the most part, have offered a good hedge against the inflationary price rises of the recent past. The value of a farm tends to go up with inflation and with rises in the prices of farm commodities.

Since 1940, farm real estate has increased an average of more than 50 per cent in terms of "real" value today. That trend is likely to continue as more good farmland is taken for highways, housing, shopping centers and other nonfarm uses. But many inexperienced people have lost money on farm operations. Again, prudence is required. It is wise to consult an established real estate agent in your community before buying property.

Income Property—An office building or an apartment building can be a good hedge against inflation. It can retain or even increase its value over the years while providing the owner with regular income from rents, which generally have risen. Again, it's important to be careful and to get expert advice. Investment properties require much know-how in selection and purchase.

The Duplex—Some people, approaching retirement, have found it worthwhile to buy a duplex or a small apartment building. The idea is to use one unit for living quarters and rent the other for income.

Resort Property—Lots or cottages on an ocean, lake or river are likely to prove increasingly attractive as a hedge against inflation. People with more leisure and longer vacations are seeking vacation spots in increasing numbers. Here, too, the location is very important.

Stocks and Bonds—In general, ownership of common stocks has turned out to be an effective safeguard against the declining value of the dollar. Stocks, in many cases, provide current income in the form of dividends and increase in value so as to keep up with or even keep ahead of the advance of inflation (see chart on page 67). Owners of bonds, in a period of declining purchasing power, have fared less well.

Borrowers—The man who borrows money and repays his debt in dollars which are declining in purchasing power tends to come out ahead in a time of inflation. In effect, he is returning dollars of lesser value for the dollars of greater value which he originally received.

The man who lends money, generally speaking, comes out the loser in a period of inflation. Both the dollars he receives as interest and the dollars of the loan which eventually is paid back to him will have declined in purchasing power as prices advanced. His only protection: Raising the interest rate charged on loans.

Money in bank accounts could be highly vulnerable to inflation. The dollar that was set aside in 1940 is worth only about 41 cents in terms of what it will buy today. The interest on dollars in savings accounts has not been sufficient to offset the rising level of prices.

Two decades of more or less continuous inflation indicate that there is no foolproof method of defense. It's just not possible to be assured of a safe position at all times and under all circumstances.

The young marrieds

Still, there are certain courses of action that can help prevent losses—or even bring the investor out ahead. Take, for example, the case of Tom Brown.

Tom Brown is a college graduate, a high-school teacher

in the public-school system in Washington, D.C. His starting salary is $6,500 a year. His wife, Nancy, works as a secretary in a publishing house. She earns $3,600 a year.

The Browns lived in a high-rise efficiency apartment where they paid rent of $185 a month. They were acutely aware that this was money gone forever. They wanted to buy a house, as a hedge against inflation, but they lacked the cash reserve for a down payment.

On top of that, the lease on Tom Brown's apartment has only six months to run. The Browns feared that, caught as they were in the inflationary spiral, the landlord might raise the rent.

So the Browns made a critical decision. With Nancy's concurrence, Tom made up his mind that, come what may, he would buy a house.

It took some belt tightening. Tom had to borrow $1,500 at the bank, but the Browns were able to make a $3,000 down payment on an $18,000 house—and move in when their lease expired.

What did this do to the Browns financially?

First, it reduced their basic outlay for living quarters. Tom had to pay the prevailing six and one half per cent interest on his $15,000 first mortgage, but even then the monthly payments were only $111.84. Real-estate taxes were another $20 a month. His monthly payments on the $1,500 loan for five years were $29.35. Thus, his total monthly outlay for mortgage payments and taxes was $161.19—as compared with $185 in the rented apartment.

True, Tom ran into new expenditures in the form of

electricity and heating bills, but these were minor when compared to the advantages he gained.

Tom had done his homework before he bought the house. He chose a house in an area on the upswing, with values rising. He looked into the school situation, found that elementary and high schools in his neighborhood had excellent ratings and were within walking distance. This assured Tom of good and convenient schools for any children he and Nancy might have. And it also helped assure excellent resale value on the house should they move to another city.

Nancy was a big help to Tom in determining whether they should buy this $18,000 house. Together they checked into such items as supermarkets and drugstores in the neighborhood, roads, water, sewer facilities and taxes. In every respect, they found the area to be satisfactory.

The young couple also followed sound advice when they actually took on more house than they needed— perhaps even more house than they could afford. They chose a house with three bedrooms and a den. Tom reasoned this way: It's better to buy plenty of house. If the family grows, it won't be necessary to add additional rooms or move to a larger house.

Most people, Tom felt, could count on rising incomes during a period of inflation. So, in effect, the Browns would be paying off their mortgage with dollars which came easier every year. Unlike the situation they faced in the apartment, the Browns were assured that their mortgage payments would not be increased. They had no assurance of continued, fixed monthly ependitures while waiting for their apartment lease to expire.

One of the biggest advantages came at the end of each year. When Tom got around to filing his annual income tax return, he was able to deduct every cent he had paid in interest on his mortgage and for real estate taxes.

Over all, as the value of Tom's home goes up and as his home loan is reduced, his equity in that home goes up. If Tom decides in the future to teach in another city, he can expect to turn enough profit on the sale of his house to buy comparable quarters elsewhere—and have something left over, too.

By taking the plunge, Tom and Nancy secured a primary hedge against inflation—buying a house.

It's not the whole answer, but more often than not it helps.

The off-beat investments

For the family with above-average means and sophisticated tastes, there are today some unique opportunities to counteract the annual fall in the purchasing power of the dollar.

It takes some special know-how and a bit of daring. If you have that, you might want to look into the possibility of investing in rare books, works of art, gold and silver coins, presidential autographs and stamp collections.

It's against the law for Americans to speculate in gold bars—to buy this precious metal in the belief that the official price of $35 an ounce will be increased, perhaps to as much as $70, offering a chance to make a big profit. The maximum penalty for this type of speculation is ten years in jail and a $10,000 fine.

But the law says nothing about speculating in gold

coins—meaning coins minted prior to 1933, so long as they are collectors' items. A small group of experts is working this field very carefully in search of unusual coins. One really successful find can solve the expert collector's inflationary problems for a long, long time.

Take the case of the New York collector who picked up a 1,700-year-old Roman coin for $200 in 1940. Late in 1967, the same coin was sold for $13,500.

The sky seems to be the limit on rare gold coins. An old U.S. $20 gold piece remains a favorite with collectors. At the end of 1968 such coins were selling for $75.

Parchment land deeds, issued to Western settlers in the nineteenth century, have proved very profitable to collectors. The reason: most of these deeds were signed personally by American Presidents of that period—notably, John Quincy Adams, Andrew Jackson and Benjamin Harrison.

A New York collector of land deeds said:

"The 100 deeds I now own cost me only $5 to $25 each and are worth up to ten times more today because of the rising demand for rare presidential autographs."

In New York department stores, land deeds signed by early American Presidents are now selling for $150 and up. They are said to offer the purchaser excellent protection against inflation.

Similarly, stamps, rare books and paintings offer special opportunities for big returns on investment. A partner in a Wall Street brokerage house declared:

"In the last seven years, I purchased fourteen paintings by lesser-known artists of the postimpressionist school. They have increased at least 150 per cent in value. I bought a landscape painted by Louis Valtat of France for only $900 in 1963 and sold it for $2,800 in 1966."

There are, of course, some obvious dangers. Those who are not experts can get into trouble. Often, objects of art cannot be cashed in quickly. You need patience—and you need to know your market. But the rewards can be great if the investor knows what he is doing.

Antiques

Another highly unusual but increasingly popular means of fighting inflation is through investment in antiques.

The market for valuable antiques is booming as never before. Prices keep climbing. It's all a part of the search for solid investments to protect cash reserves. The facts are these—

In price appreciation, antique furniture and decorative objects are now outrunning most paintings, precious metals, diamonds and most stocks.

Purchases of antiques increasingly are being made as a hedge against inflation. Buyers believe that good antiques are certain to go up in real value and to increase in price more than enough to offset the falling value of the dollar. The supply of antiques is limited—and dwindling. The demand is increasing, both from individuals and museums.

Under U.S. law, antiques are defined as objects having been made before the year 1830.

If purchased abroad, properly certified antiques may be brought into the United States free of duty. For many years now, touring Americans have browsed through the second-hand shops in Munich, Vienna, London, Rome and Paris looking for objects of art which somehow escaped the sharp eyes of the experts.

Much of the time, the tourists come away with worthless merchandise or pretentious fakes. Now and again, however, someone strikes it rich.

Dr. Franz Pick of New York City, an economist and a leading authority on purchases of foreign currency, says that people in general buy antiques "for conservation of assets—not for esthetics."

The antiques market came into existence on a world scale about 50 years ago, Dr. Pick declared, at the beginning of what he called the period of "debasement of currency."

Dr. Pick makes these points about antiques—

Antiques can easily be transferred from one country to another; currencies often cannot be.

Ancient objects maintain or increase their value; money values decline. Antiques can be sold anonymously. That appeals, Dr. Pick suggested, to those who like to use a numbered Swiss bank account because of its guarantee of anonymity.

How much do prices of antiques appreciate? Here are some recent examples—

A Louis XVI commode, purchased at auction in New York City in 1949 for $2,500, was sold in London for $22,400 in 1963.

A Louis XV lacquered bureau, bought for $2,500 in 1941, was sold in 1965 for 20 times that amount.

An English-made silver tray of the George I era, sold for $2,200 in the early '30s, was resold in 1966 for $15,000.

A pair of George II circular cake baskets, thought by

some experts to be copies, were sold to a New York dealer for $500 in 1961. The dealer had a hunch the cake baskets were originals. When they were authenticated in 1963, they sold for $43,400.

In London, which considers itself the capital of the antiques market, the trade's explosive growth is attributed to the expansion of the middle class in much of the world.

A British dealer observed:

"More and more people everywhere have idle money on their hands. They want to buy something that will be admired by their friends and will hold its value. They turn to antiques."

The antique field is also remunerative for the small-time investor, as the figures for these recent transactions show—

A porcelain tiger figurine which cost $266 in 1949 was sold in 1966 for $4,200. And a hand-carved paperweight, picked up in a junk store in Munich in 1960 for $10, turned out to be early Italian and fetched $1,500 at a London auction in 1965.

What are some of the best objects to buy for investment? A survey of dealers turns up these items—

Porcelain. Still very big.

Furniture. Good but tricky. Many pieces don't "travel" well, suffer from climate in the U.S.

Antique transparent glass. Consult an expert.

Silverware. A solid investment in most cases.

Pistols. An old standby. If authentic, you can hardly go wrong.

Gold, silver and jade objects from Indian civilizations of pre-Christian times.

African art items. Coming on fast now.

All this should be considerably tempered with words of warning. For the amateur, investment buying of antiques is full of pitfalls. Trends in the market change quickly. Even experts may make mistakes in judgment.

Howard L. Katzander, publisher of "International Art Market" in New York, said:

"People who buy only for investment often are disappointed and feel that they have been misled. It's a question of trying to anticipate the public's taste, which is not easy."

Most of the professionals agree that the odds against finding a real prize at an auction are growing longer all the time. When something of exceptional quality is about to be auctioned, dealers often form a syndicate to buy it. The syndicate then can dispose of the object, with each member realizing some profit, rather than bidding against one another until the price is "out of sight."

It is estimated that there are now more than 20,000 antique dealers in the United States. That compares with 14,000 just eight years ago.

What do the dealers think of the antiques market in general?

Almost to a man, they agree on this: "The only way the market can go is up."

That doesn't mean, however, that satisfaction—or profit—is guaranteed. From the experts, you get these tips:

If you are contemplating a costly acquisition, it is well

to seek the services of a connoisseur who can gauge the real and potential value of the item you wish to buy.

Aspiring collectors should "read up" on fields in which they are interested—crystal, porcelain, silverware or furniture, for example.

In all of these fields, values are increasing rapidly. But the person who has done his homework will find that many pieces of great or potential value are still available for comparatively modest outlays.

What businessmen do

For the businessman, inflation, of course, poses a serious problem. Today he must take these points into account: There has been more or less continuous inflation in the United States since World War II. After 1965, the rate of inflation increased. For 1967 it was 3 per cent; for 1968, over 4 per cent. Thereafter, it may conceivably decline to around 2 per cent a year. If so, that would mean about a 25 per cent rise in prices over the ten years between 1967 and 1977.

With the possibility that about one-fourth of the dollar's buying power may vanish in the next decade, prudent businessmen must plan accordingly.

The firm's top man must retain the key executives of his firm, and see to it that they are not lost to competitors who offer better rewards. If this means paying higher salaries, it could still prove less expensive than hiring and training replacements.

Some companies invest part of the income of their key employes until their retirement. This gives top men long-range security and discourages their leaving for other positions.

If a company is growing, it may want to act on expansion plans and to get a new building program underway. Prices of labor and materials are high, but they will go higher. So will land costs for a plant site in and around major cities.

Whatever is put into construction or equipment now is almost sure to represent a saving over what the same services and material will cost in 1969 or 1970. Besides, building now at present-day prices may offer the advantage of paying off the construction bill later with "cheaper" dollars as the inflationary trend continues.

What about stocks on hand—inventories? Some managers believe it wise to build up a larger reserve at current prices. It is possible to get hurt if inventories are too low. A good stockpile can bring handsome rewards if there is a sudden advance in prices.

Here again, borrowing holds a special attraction. Borrowed money, devoted to plant expansion or higher inventories, may be repaid later with "cheaper" dollars—and interest charges are tax-deductible.

These, then, are some of the means available to individuals and business enterprises to shield themselves from the effects of inflation. One of the most important—investment in stocks—deserves a separate chapter.

CHAPTER FIVE

The Investor in Times of Inflation

It is almost certain that, regardless of the political party in power, the national debt contracted by the U. S. Government will keep getting bigger. And it is also likely that inflation will pose a challenge to investors for a long time to come.

Today's dollar has less value in terms of what it will buy than at any time in American history.

Still, the record of this century holds some comfort for the investor who wishes to protect himself. It is significant that in the last 50 years, while the dollar was shrinking in value by more than one half, the people who put their money in good-quality common stocks not only preserved the real value of their capital but also increased it.

And they achieved this result even when they bought their stock at the high price levels of 1929, 1937 and 1946.

There is no guarantee that stocks will continue to act so favorably in the future. There is always a chance that market investments may not prove as effective in hedging against inflation as they have in the past. But it may be unwise to assume that there is nothing to be learned from the performance of common stocks during periods of inflation in the twentieth century.

When you hedge against inflation you put a solid part of your assets into holdings that you feel will rise in dollar value as prices rise.

Some, of an extremely cautious nature, may regard this as a form of gambling, and at first glance, it may look that way. On closer inspection, however, it appears that those who take a moderate, calculated risk are often more successful in conserving their capital than those who do not.

If one sticks to investments which promise a limited but secure return, he is, in effect, *betting* that prices are not going to go up faster than the modest earnings on the investments. That's a real gamble!

Investments in sound stocks of companies with strong growth potentials, on the other hand, may prove less risky. If prices in general fall, growth stocks tend to hold up. And in times of boom, such stocks usually outrun the rising prices.

An inflation hedge is best geared to a long-term goal. It takes into consideration the trends over a 10-year period, rather than the special situations in which one might make a quick profit.

Those who hedge successfully say that they diversify —or spread out their investments. By doing so, they spread their risks. Thus, they reduce the danger of loss while pursuing gains which more than offset losses in the value of the dollar as a result of inflation.

CHANGES IN STOCK PRICES SINCE 1939

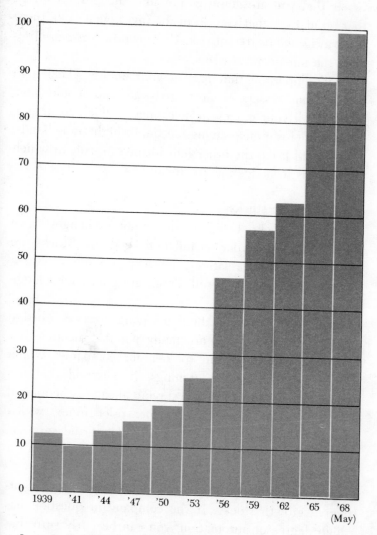

Source: Standard & Poor's 500 Stocks. 1941-43 = 10

To do this, you must first decide the *proportion* of your assets that you are going to put into "hedges," realizing that no matter what you do in the investment field, there is always *some* degree of risk. Unknown factors can upset even the most careful plans.

So it's important that part of your holdings be left in highly secure assets. Some experts say you should have at least half your money in investments which are highly secure—life insurance, savings accounts, high-grade bonds. That would leave the other half for investments in which your aim is to hedge against inflation.

Choosing your stocks

Common stocks, listed on the major exchanges, have proved highly popular as inflation "hedges." Stocks are easily acquired, at relatively low expense. They offer a ready market when you sell. Prices are public knowledge every day.

What do you look for, then, in buying stocks as a hedge against inflation? There are many popular theories, but in general, it's important to look for companies which show good increases in earnings. If you find that the earnings of certain stocks are staying ahead of the annual rise in the Government's consumer price index, which measures the rise or fall of prices of goods and services, these stocks might seriously be considered as a haven for your capital.

There are other factors to consider in picking out attractive growth stocks. If the company in question has a high degree of automation, you can be fairly sure that labor costs are going to be held in check. It naturally follows that those companies which are automated are likely to be in a stronger position than those which are not.

If the company, because of its location or other factors, is able to operate with minimum staff, you again have an efficient situation which should make its stock attractive to those who seek capital growth over the long term.

From the preceding analysis it follows that some of the best hedges against inflation will be found in the common stocks of companies in these activities:

Automated and business equipment.
Chemicals.
Electrical equipment.
Electric and gas utilities.
Investment.
Oil.
Paper and paper containers.
Tires and rubber.

Mutual funds

To those who prefer to let professional managers handle their investments in a diversified portfolio of common stocks and other securities, mutual funds may be of interest.

How does a mutual fund work? Suppose that you and a few friends put $100 each into a pool so that you could share in the purchase of a greater number of different stocks than each could buy individually. With little experience in the market, your group might hire a professional to advise you on what stocks to buy. Depending on how the stock market was acting and on your professional's

GROWTH-TYPE MUTUAL FUNDS
How $10,000, invested January 1, 1958,
grew in value, with Capital-Gains Dividends Reinvested.

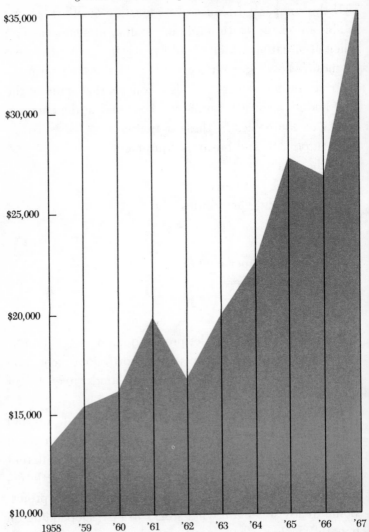

judgment, the value of your investment would then go up or down.

Basically, that is the way a mutual fund operates.

Today, nearly 4 million Americans have invested in more than 300 mutual funds. Their investment is estimated to be about $50 billion.

Those Americans are confident that this nation's industry will continue to expand and that, by sharing in its future, their dollars will grow and will meet or outrun the cost of inflation.

Land as an investment

There is still another type of investment which has proved to be sound in times of inflation: real estate stocks. There is plenty of evidence to suggest that land will continue to be an ideal inflation hedge and companies with large real estate holdings will benefit substantially as prices continue to rise.

The main reason land offers such a good investment is that, for all practical purposes, the amount of land is fixed while the demand for land increases. It is, of course, true that land may be reclaimed through draining or filling large areas, but such operations are expensive and have little real effect on the overall supply.

As new families are formed, there is less and less land to go around. Furthermore, since land is one of the basic requirements for production, it follows that continued economic growth will demand more and more land.

Nearly all forms of activity are based on land. There is no substitute for it. Land yields natural resources—natural gas, minerals, oil, timber. The demand for usable land, generally, can go only one way: up. The value of such land must also go up.

Looking for growth

In general, finding the stocks which have the best potential for long-term growth is really just a matter of common sense. Take a look around at the country's problems. Consider, for example, water pollution.

The amount of water used per person has quadrupled since 1900 while the population has almost tripled. An estimated 65 per cent of the fresh water in populated areas is choked with sewage and industrial waste. Huge federal programs have been enacted providing vast sums to build treatment plants.

The Department of Commerce estimated that $25 billion will be spent in the next 10 years to restore our water supply. Private industry will bear the major share of the burden. Capital expenditures for water treatment are on the order of $2 billion a year; almost that much is to be spent annually on waste treatment. Over the next five years, these expenditures are expected to climb 20 per cent a year.

Take a look, now, at a related field: converting salt water to drinking water. The Department of the Interior expects the use of world-wide desalting techniques to go up dramatically. Early in 1968, only 120 million gallons of water per day were being reclaimed from the sea. By 1972, the figure is expected to reach 1.2 *billion* gallons per day.

There are no longer any technological barriers to the

conversion of sea water to fresh water. The problem now is cost. Desalting water still costs a dollar for each 1,000 gallons. That is down from $4 per 1,000 gallons just a few years ago. But it is still too expensive compared with the ordinary cost of delivering fresh water.

That is not going to stop American industry from conquering this problem. Investors are keeping a sharp eye on the industrial approach to all the problems of water supply.

Similarly, the fields of communications, computers and data processing, air freight, passenger travel, clean air and many others offer opportunities to the investor who wants to put his money in America's future.

Mining stocks still have a strong attraction for many investors. One American put $100,000 into five U. S. and Canadian gold-mining companies in 1960. His investment tripled in value in six years. He felt it was a good hedge against a possible drop in the value of the dollar.

Similarly, the growing scarcity of silver and the increased demand for silver by industry made silver stocks popular again.

One investor tells of putting $20,000 into four silver-mining companies in the course of the four years ended in January, 1968. By then, the stock was worth $30,000. Many investment authorities say that a well-balanced portfolio of stocks should include precious metals. It should be remembered that metal stocks can be highly volatile. They can go down or way up.

Another investor had exceptional luck in buying farm-land near an expanding highway system. And one man who bought up interests in active oil wells in 1963 got earnings of nearly 100 per cent on his investment.

In short, dealing successfully with inflation is a matter of buying something that will go up in value as the purchasing power of the dollar goes down. The challenge is to find the investment which is more than a match for inflation.

CHAPTER SIX

What Causes Inflation?

Who's to blame for sending prices up? And why did he do it?

Everyone claims to be innocent. Each person points to the next.

The butcher says it's the baker.

The baker says it's the candlestick maker.

And the candlestick maker says it's the butcher.

Whoever started it (and we'll find the culprits later), one thing is certain: Sooner or later, everyone gets into the act.

Whether it was the butcher who first raised the price of his beef, or the baker who raised the price of his bread, or the candlestick maker who raised the price of his candles, the fact is that all three raised their prices.

All three, perhaps apologetically and wearing long faces, will explain to grumbling customers that their costs were going up and up, and they simply had to raise their prices—or go out of business.

The customer may go on grumbling; but he has to go on buying if he wants meat, bread and candles because all retailers and producers are raising their prices. There may be small differences among them—accented by week-end sales of special items which are artificially reduced as a "come-on" to lure in customers—but prices generally are higher.

The reason merchants give usually is a good one—their costs *are* going up.

How prices rise

Assume you are the baker. If the price of the flour from the miller goes up; if the cost of delivering it from the wholesaler to your bakery goes up; if the cost of your gas and electricity goes up, if the wages of your employe who minds the oven go up, you will have to charge your customer more for your bread—or go broke.

What about the trucker who delivers the flour? The price of his tires had just gone up. The cost of his gasoline and oil had also gone up. The cost of the truck itself had just gone up because the manufacturers in Detroit had raised their prices. He *had* to raise his price for delivering the flour or he, too, would have had to go out of business.

The next day, when he learned that the price of the loaf of bread his wife brought home had been increased, he began to wonder whether he had raised his delivery charge enough. In time, when prices kept going up for all the items consumed by his family and all the items involved in his business, he stopped wondering and raised his own prices again.

Why did the manufacturers of the truck raise their

prices? For the same reason. All their costs were going up, too—labor, steel, aluminum, tires, electricity and all the other elements that go into making a truck.

Every truck and every bus that came out of Detroit at a higher price eventually had the effect of raising the cost of moving every commodity transported by truck and every passenger carried by that bus. In short, the costs went up for almost anything and anyone that moved— and that covered almost everything and everyone in the country.

The producers of steels, aluminum, tires, electricity and all the other elements that went into making the truck had the same explanation as the Detroit manufacturers—all *their* costs had gone up, too.

Workers in these and all other industries, in raising the price of their labor, had the same explanation—*their* cost of living had gone up.

Once the prices of the ingredients of life start going up —bread, meat, milk, eggs—and once the prices of the ingredients of manufactured goods go up—labor, steel, rubber, wood, electricity—then the prices of everything inevitably go up. The cost of making one product enters into the cost of making another. And labor enters into all of them.

Once prices start bumping each other up, the spiraling "dance" of prices is under way, and no butcher, baker or candlestick maker can stop it.

We still don't know who started it. So far, it seems that no one did—or everyone did.

If you want to establish how deep the mystery and confusion is throughout the nation (and the entire world, for that matter), you need simply ask the next few people you meet if they can tell you who or what was responsible for the rising prices and the inflation about which everyone always complains.

Notwithstanding the difficulty in identifying the culprits, they are visible to the public every day, and the landscape is littered with their footprints.

The money supply

You may recall our definition of the word "inflation" as applied to money—"an unusual 'swelling' or expansion of the supply of money relative to the supply of goods and services."

Who expands the money supply?

At the outset, you need to keep in mind what makes up the nation's money supply. There's "jingle" money (coins), "folding" money (paper currency) and "check-book" money (money on deposit in checking accounts in banks).

Coins and paper money in circulation—the $1, $2, $5, $10, $20, $50, and $100 bills—make up only about 20 per cent of the money supply. Money in checking accounts makes up the lion's share of today's money. People find that checks are readily accepted, can serve as receipts and involve less risk of loss than does cash. Bankers estimate that checks pay for 90 per cent of the total dollar volume of transactions in the United States. Coin and currency account for only 10 per cent.

Checks, thus, do most of the work that money does in our economy. It's "check-book money," too, that plays a key role when the supply of money in the country is expanded.

For example, let's assume you need to borrow $1,000 to help pay college costs for your son. You apply for a loan at your local bank and, because your credit is good, the bank approves the loan.

Now, when the bank advances the money it will not give you ten $100 bills. Rather, it will credit your checking account for $1,000—against which you can draw a check to pay your son's college fees.

Your local bank, thus, has "created" $1,000 which has been added to the nation's money supply. Note, however, that this is not a one-way street. When you repay the loan, the bank will "extinguish" the $1,000 deposit it had made and thus reduce the money supply.

The important point to remember is that when commercial banks make loans and investments they add to the money supply in our economy.

With that in mind, are banks the inflation culprit? No, not all. Banking laws—at the Federal and State level—give banks the power to "create" money. A smoothly-functioning economy requires credit facilities to meet needs of business, Government and consumers in a growing, changing country. Remember, in our example, that it was the local bank that got you over the financial squeeze brought on by college expenses.

The role of government

We have to look elsewhere in our inflation "whodunit."

The major cause, most economists agree, is excessive spending by the Government in Washington. When the

Government spends more than it takes in from taxes, the result is "red ink"—a deficit. That deficit has to be covered by loans. Such borrowing can, and often does, increase the money supply and add to inflation pressures.

It's the same process we noted above. The Government goes to banks to borrow money to cover its deficit. It raises the money by selling securities to the banks. The banks, in turn, pay for the bonds by crediting the Government's checking account. Money is "created," moves into the spending stream as the Government pays out the money to meet expenses.

Government deficits, to be sure, need not necessarily add to the money supply and aggravate inflation. When the Government raises money by selling its bonds or other securities to people or to companies, such borrowings are not inflationary. People and businesses draw on their savings to buy the bonds, thus reducing their spending power.

But when the Government runs heavy and repeated "red ink" in the budget, it cannot raise all the money it needs by tapping savings of people and business. It's forced to resort to borrowing from banks—and that's when the money supply expands. Money then begins "chasing" goods. The inflation spiral begins to twist upward.

When Government lives beyond its means, thus, it tends to feed inflation.

When are such problems most acute for Government? Above all, in time of war. Costs of waging war send Government expenditures skyrocketing. The costs are so great that they cannot be completely covered by dollars in the form of taxes or loans from people or business.

To make up the difference between its needs and usual revenues, the Government, in effect, "turns on the printing presses" and secures billions of dollars which it uses as freely and as easily as dollars secured from taxes, war bonds and other loans.

Consider what happened during the Vietnam War. As our involvement became deeper and deeper and we increased the number of our troops in the field to more than 500,000 men, expenditures of the Defense Department moved up accordingly. At the same time, the Johnson Administration felt committed to its "Great Society" programs, and even proposed to increase them after racial rioting broke out across the country.

This involved a double burden running into unprecedented billions of dollars each year, and the annual budgets of the Johnson Administration were the highest in the nation's history.

The bill for everything the Government proposed to spend came to much more than the Government was getting from taxes. There was one solution—the one used throughout history in circumstances of this kind: the "printing press."

In the old days the Government literally ordered its own printing presses to turn out the additional mountains of dollar bills it needed to cover its deficits. This became too easy and too dangerous a habit. Measures were devised to impede this practice by the Government and thereby protect the dollars held by the people from being depreciated by a deluge of freshly printed bills.

Now, in order to get ready cash of this kind, the Government must operate through the Federal Reserve System—the nation's central bank—and the commercial banks, issuing bonds in exchange for the fresh supplies of money and credit (more on the Federal Reserve's role in a later chapter). This may be less crude than the old-fashioned system, but it can produce similar results. We have, in effect, the "printing press" in more sophisticated form.

Under this system, the Government in recent years secured billions of dollars. Some were turned over to the Defense Department, which handed them out to all the companies with which it had contracts for the manufacture of bombers, fighter planes, guns, bullets, jeeps, ships, clothing and food for the troops and the other thousands upon thousands of items that go into the waging of war.

Other billions of dollars were turned over to the Department of Health, Education and Welfare, which distributed them to the different States to help upgrade education and to different agencies throughout the country to try to improve the lot of the poor and disadvantaged. Still other amounts were turned over to the Department of Housing and Urban Development for the war against urban blight. And so on, down through all the various federal agencies.

These dollars, in cash or checks, were indistinguishable from other dollars, and were accepted by the manufacturers of war goods, books and housing as readily as any others.

The workers and employes of war industries, in turn, received and spent these dollars as if they were the same as any others. So did all those who worked in the nation's schools and in the construction industry.

But, as indicated earlier, these dollars were *not* really

the same. They were what we might call "Government deficit dollars." They reflected the Government's budget deficit, which exceeded $25 billion in 1968.

These "deficit dollars" did *not* represent goods which had been produced, yet they enabled the Government to buy goods which were in the market.

When it is waging wars and conducting antipoverty programs with the approval of the Congress and the people, the Government may be financing its budget deficits in the only practical way left open to it—by "inflating" the currency.

This practice sometimes is also described as "watering down" or "diluting" the currency because when "worthless" money (in the sense of paper that does not represent production of goods and services) is mixed with "good" money (meaning dollars which *do* represent such production), the value of the "good" money must go down as prices go up.

Economists have coined a phrase to describe what happens in such a situation. They call it "demand-pull" inflation because an increased demand for goods in limited supply "pulls" up the prices for these goods.

Whatever tag one chooses to put on it, the net result is the same—rising prices and consequently falling value of the dollar.

The story of swollen budgets, huge deficits covered by artificial "paper" currency and consequent inflation is the story of all nations and Governments involved in major wars throughout history.

It was the story of our greatest spurts in prices on seven occasions of U.S. history—the Revolutionary War, the War of 1812, the Civil War, two world wars, the Korean War and the Vietnam War.

The financing of wartime deficits with "paper" dollars, if one stops to think about it, is the equivalent of imposing additional taxes on the people without appearing to do so. The declining value of money is not as readily apparent to the people as are taxes—and hence inflation seems less painful.

The pain, however, soon makes itself felt. This may not apply so much in the case of working people and others whose rising wages and incomes help counteract the decline in the purchasing power of money. But those who have accumulated savings and who live on fixed pensions are severely squeezed.

Inflation is called the "cruelest tax of all" because it penalizes those who saved money in the belief that money would preserve its value (and the Government would not debase it), and it deals a blow to those least able to take it—the aged and the infirm, living on fixed incomes.

The role of labor and business

Government—the principal actor in the inflation drama —is not the only one.

A share of the blame can be attributed to another form of inflation—the loss of value sustained by our currency when a worker is given a raise which pays him for more than he has produced, or when companies take advantage of shortages or heavy demand by customers to make profits which are an excessively high return on invested capital.

If a labor union, through its monopoly bargaining power, insists on getting raises for its members which exceed the increased output per man-hour, then it might be said that the workers are getting something for nothing, and someone will have to pay for it.

We the people, of course, have to pay for such raises in the form of higher prices for goods on the market, as businessmen pass on increased costs.

Members of labor unions deny that their raises are "inflationary" and argue that they are simply taking a share of the greater profits earned by their companies. Figures indicate, nevertheless, that wage increases in many industries have exceeded increases in worker productivity.

Wages were increased 6 per cent and more during 1967 and 1968. Increased output per man-hour was estimated at only about half that much. Result: higher costs for business, with steady upward pressure on prices. That explains, in part, why we must pay more pennies and dollars for almost everything we buy. We are paying for what workers are buying with wages they did not earn through increased production.

Economists, again, have a special phrase to describe this kind of inflation. They call it "cost-push"—because higher costs (such as the increased cost of labor) push up the prices of goods.

Again, whatever one calls it, the results are rising prices and declining value of the dollar.

We have now identified the factors primarily responsible for sending up prices: large and persistent Government budget deficits; workers who force excessive wage gains; and companies which take higher profits than are regarded as reasonable.

If a country wants stable money, its people must see

to it that their spending does not exceed what they earn through production, and its Government must learn to live within its income.

CHAPTER SEVEN

Inflation — and the Cost of Governing

All Governments in America—Federal, State and city— face this common problem: A rising demand for more and better public services and the hard reality that there isn't enough money to foot the bills.

One of the reasons Government cannot cope is the steady upward movement of costs brought on by inflation. It is also true that as population increases, so do the costs for governing that growing population, but the effects of *inflation alone* are so severe that many Governments are getting by today on a hand-to-mouth basis.

To get an idea of what the Federal Government is up against, consider the pressures of inflation in only one field: waging the war in Vietnam.

Figures released by the U.S. Bureau of the Budget tell this story—

Back in 1954, when France was defeated at Dienbienphu and we had not yet become deeply involved in Vietnam, the United States had a national defense budget

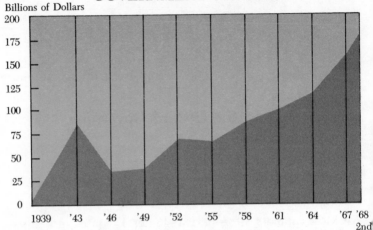

TRENDS IN FEDERAL
GOVERNMENT SPENDING

Billions of Dollars

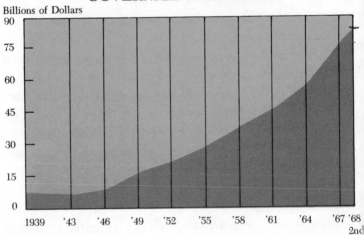

TRENDS IN STATE & LOCAL
GOVERNMENT SPENDING

Billions of Dollars

Source: U.S. Department of Commerce.

of nearly $47 billion. This was more than 65 per cent of the total budget.

By 1968, the war in Vietnam had raised defense expenditures to more than $80 billion. This represented 45 per cent of the total budget.

Hidden within these figures, however, are inflationary pressures. Everything, from a single round of rifle ammunition to the latest jet fighter, costs a great deal more than it did 5, or 10 or 15 years ago.

For example, take a military jeep, which has not changed very much from models used in earlier wars. A jeep today costs the Government $2,700—compared to $2,200 during the Korean War. Or consider the cost of a soldier's uniform. Today it's $61, as against only $40 as recently as 16 years ago. Pay of fighting men, too, has gone up. Today a buck private is paid $109.50 a month—up 32 per cent since Korean War days.

Such figures, of course, tell only part of the story. There is no way to figure accurately how much inflationary increase in price there is in a jet fighter. Certainly there is no way of comparing the cost of an F-86—the American plane the Free Chinese used against MIG 15s and 17s in the dogfights above the China Straits in the late 1950s—and today's F-111s.

Today's planes, vastly more expensive, are also more highly developed. The cost of all weaponry went up because the weapons are more efficient and technically more advanced. That tends to obscure the fact that the rising costs of parts and labor and contractual services have played a big hand in what weapons are costing the American taxpayer now.

An inside glimpse into what rising costs have done to the defense budget was provided by the running battle over the controversial plane known as tactical fighter experimental (TFX). During the several years that Congress debated whether or not to build the TFX, the price of the aircraft—on the drawing board—advanced from $4 million to about $12 million.

State and local governments suffer similar problems. A special study indicated that spending by State and local governments in 1966 would double by 1975. These governments spent about $75 billion in 1966. The figure is expected to come close to $150 billion by 1975.

There is nothing particularly new or startling in this trend. The States have been wrestling with the cost of living—and piling up big debts—ever since the end of World War II.

The total debt of State and local governments in 1945 was $13.7 billion. In 1967, it came to $113.4 billion—an increase of 728 per cent. During the same period, the Federal Government's debt increased by 18 per cent.

Inflation's assault on our cities

Let's take a look at what it costs to run seven major American cities on a per capita basis. In other words, let's examine the costs of running these cities in terms of money spent annually for each individual of the city's total population.

These were the per capita appropriations for the year 1967:

New York City	$560.23
Los Angeles	$471.87
Rochester	$436.03
Detroit	$365.35
Chicago	$358.04
Philadelphia	$350.63
Buffalo	$339.61

New York City's per capita outlay was only $186 in 1953. By 1962 it climbed 81 per cent—to $337.

Similarly, the figure for Los Angeles went up 69 per cent—from $221 to $373 between 1953 and 1962.

Chicago showed an even higher rate of advance for the same period, from $135 per person to $334 per person —or a 147 per cent increase.

Philadelphia spent $243 per person in 1962, compared with $136 in 1953. In Detroit, over the same period, expenditures rose from $160 to $311.

Spending more and more money, however, did not solve the problems. The cities remained crowded. Neighborhoods ran downhill. The more affluent city residents fled to the suburbs—eroding the tax base which cities could tap. At the same time, there was growing demand for welfare services and police protection. Transportation systems broke down. Schools became hard pressed to handle the increasing number of pupils. Costs of running cities rose all along the line.

Almost without fail, mayors, city managers and city councils complained during the middle '60s that inflation was a major headache.

Solutions were hard to come by. It wasn't for lack of

trying. Across the country, the pattern was the same. Real estate taxes went up. Sales taxes were added. Many cities adopted income taxes, raised water taxes. Still, the new revenue was no match for the soaring city budgets caught in the inflation swirl.

Nowhere was this more apparent than in the field of average salaries paid to city workers. The most dramatic example, in all likelihood, is New York City.

In 1947, the average salary paid to an employe of the City of New York was $3,352. By 1953, the figure had inched up to $4,162. It jumped to $5,380 in 1957 and to $5,970 in 1962.

But an even steeper rise was yet to come. In 1967, the average pay of a city employe in New York was $7,574. In store, because of continuing pressures of inflation, is more of the same.

Over the period 1946 to 1966, the outstanding indebtedness of New York City rose from $1.2 billion to $2.7 billion. This increase in debt took place despite a sharp rise in real-estate taxes of nearly one dollar for each $100 of assessed valuation between 1954 and 1967. Increases in real-estate taxes, a rise from 15 to 20 cents for a subway ride and the introduction of a lottery were measures which served only to limit—but not to dam up—the forces of inflation.

One New York official put it this way—

"The mayor is doing a great job against overwhelming odds. It is quite possible that nobody can really successfully govern this city. In degree, our problems are more severe than the problems facing the nation.

"Look at our public-welfare program, for instance. In

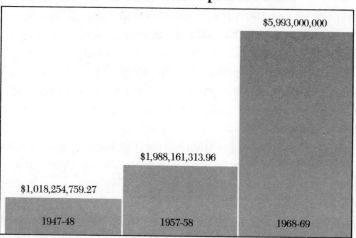

GOVERNING NEW YORK CITY
How the Cost Went Up in 21 Years

$5,993,000,000

$1,988,161,313.96

$1,018,254,759.27

1947-48   1957-58   1968-69

The Rising Cost in Some Key Categories

Category	(Budget, as adjusted, to nearest total of millions of dollars) 1947-48	1957-58	1966-67
Supplies	30	44	117
Equipment	6	5	25
Contractual Services	27	57	287
Social Welfare	147	242	719
Pensions	66	196	364
Fixed Charges	38	50	306
Debt Service	199	352	638

* 1968-69 = Proposed Estimate

January of 1966, we had 539,395 people on public assistance. A year later there were 630,000 on the rolls. By September of 1967, that figure was up above 750,000. Do you realize what that means? It means that 1 person in every 11 in New York City is on relief. Half a million are children. And it's getting worse every day.

"Look at the city payroll. Inflation is beating us to death. And all the time, the demand for more and better services keeps increasing. Then you get a situation where the sanitation workers demand and get more money and that sets off unrest among other public workers. It's a vicious circle and I for one don't know how we're going to break out of it.

"What is it going to take to run this city? Who knows? We need about $6 billion for 1969. Chances are we won't get it. Chances are, by 1969, $6 billion won't be enough. If you were to ask me what we will need, I'd say $10 billion a year is a good, round number to put everything in order for the 1970s. And if something isn't done to put a damper on inflation, that may not be enough by the time 1970 rolls around."

The accompanying charts present a picture of what has happened in the past 20 years to the cost of governing a major city like New York. The steady advance in the cost of goods, services, salaries, fees and commissions has quadrupled the cost of running New York. Better than words, these figures show how a big city can become a prime victim of inflation.

CHAPTER EIGHT

Bringing Inflation Under Control

From what we observed in earlier chapters it follows that corrective measures to stop or slow down inflation presumably will center on the following:

- Excessive expansion of the money supply often growing out of unrestrained Government spending.
- Wage increases which exceed the increased productivity of workers.
- Pricing policies of some companies that produce unreasonable profits.

The Government can reduce or eliminate its inflation-feeding deficits by cutting down on spending and increasing taxes. Leaders of Congress, in fact, have insisted that the Government cut back $6 billion in its proposed spending for the 1969 budget year as their price for granting the President's request for higher taxes.

But cutting Government spending is easier said than done, and Congressmen seldom agree among themselves as to where the cuts should be made. Many may see the need for reducing appropriations which would affect the industries and rehabilitation programs of another State, but they would have difficulty in accepting cuts affecting their own State.

Furthermore, with racial disturbances threatening the internal peace of the country, there are proposals for spending still more to meet the problem. These are of two kinds—defensive measures to curb disorders, and measures for improving the lot of the poor.

Inflation hits the Government, as a consumer, as hard as it does all other consumers. And the Government is the largest single consumer in the country.

As prices go up, it must pay more and more for new roads, housing, and cleaning up urban slums. The cost of Social Security and other social-welfare programs keeps increasing. The prospects of cutting expenditures in these areas, therefore, are not bright.

Proposals to reduce expenditures on our activities in space would save considerable sums of money, but champions of the National Aeronautics and Space Administration are constantly warning members of Congress and the public that these economies would be made at the risk of losing the space race to the Russians and at some risk to our future security.

Much of the Government's budget cannot be cut because payments are required by law—such as veterans benefits and interest on the debt.

The one great saving which could change the entire picture could come with the end of the Vietnam war. The combination of heavy war expenditures abroad and

costly social welfare programs at home made it difficult to cut costs sufficiently to correct the problem of inflation.

Increased taxes voted by Congress in 1968 were helpful in the drive against inflation. The additional dollars taken from the people and business could be used to help pay for the things Government buys, to reduce the budget deficit and to hold down additions to the money supply.

There was, however, the sobering thought that a cut in spending by the public might have the effect of slowing down the economy. With less money available to them as a result of higher taxes, consumers might tighten up on the purse strings. Stores consequently might reduce somewhat their orders from manufacturers. Manufacturers, in turn, might decide to scale back production runs, and start laying off some workers.

Rising unemployment and a slowing in the pace of expansion might broaden out—and lead to a business recesion.

Bringing the Government's budget under control, in short, carries some risks. The economy must undergo adjustments as higher taxes take hold and the Government searches for ways to cut back spending programs. Economists use the analogy of a temporary "hangover" for the economy brought on by the previous inflation binge.

However, this does not necessarily mean a business slump. Even if a setback develops, it could be relatively mild and brief, in the view of the great majority of U.S. economists.

Why the optimism?

The Federal Reserve

A major reason can be found in a handsome marble structure on Constitution Avenue in Washington, D.C. It's the home of the Federal Reserve Board—the "Supreme Court of Finance."

This powerful, though relatively little known, agency plays a big role in helping keep the U.S. economy on an even keel.

The general idea is that the Federal Reserve makes it easier for people to borrow when business is slow and harder for them to borrow when business is active.

When business is slow, and people are cautious in spending, increased availability of money and credit is intended to spur spending and create jobs.

When business is active, and jobs are abundant, less ready availability of money and credit is intended to check spending and put a damper on the tendency of prices to rise.

What is the "Fed," as it is called by bankers? And how does it exercise its power over the pocketbooks of 200 million Americans?

Congress created the Federal Reserve System back in 1913.

Congress, however, does not run it.

Neither does the President of the United States.

It is an independent organization within the Government. The intent of Congress was to keep the job of managing the nation's money free from politics and private pressures.

The Federal Reserve System is run by a Board of

Governors of seven men appointed by the President of the U.S. with the consent of the U.S. Senate. Twelve Federal Reserve Banks in different parts of the country, each with its own president and board of directors, compose the Federal Reserve System.

The relationship between the Board of Governors in Washington and 12 Reserve Banks might be compared to the relationship between the Federal Government and the various State governments.

Like the Federal Government, the Board of Governors usually concentrates on matters of national importance. Like the States, the 12 Reserve Banks tend to specialize on matters within their districts.

How, then, does the Federal Reserve System function? What are its areas of responsibility?

First, the Federal Reserve is a *central bank,* and, therefore, is not like the bank most people do business with. It won't give you a loan, and it won't accept your deposits.

It has four principal functions—

1. It is a bank for banks.
2. It is the Government's bank.
3. It supervises member banks to help them stay safe and sound.
4. It manages the nation's supply of money.

Banks need a bank for much the same reasons you and your family need a bank—to cash checks, hold deposits and make loans.

Your neighborhood bank—a commercial bank—is a retailer of banking services. In a sense, the Federal Reserve is a wholesaler. Many things it does for banks help them serve you better.

For example, the check-cashing function:

When a member bank needs cash—coin and paper money—to pay out to its customers, it may turn to the Federal Reserve. The bank can draw on its deposits with the Federal Reserve for cash, which will be shipped by armored truck or by mail. To do this job, the Federal Reserve keeps a huge supply of currency and coins in its vaults. This cash comes from the United States Treasury, where it is printed—or minted.

A paycheck is only a bit of paper. You know you can spend it by converting it to cash or depositing it in your bank and writing checks against it.

Your bank receives hundreds, even thousands, of checks every day. Your bank gives depositors credit for them and, naturally, it wants to get paid back itself. This means sending the checks back to the banks on which they are drawn.

The Federal Reserve helps the banks collect the checks they receive. It tells member banks in effect: "Bundle up your checks and send them to us. We will sort them and present them to the proper banks. When we get paid, we'll pay you."

This saves your bank the trouble and expense of sorting the checks and mailing them individually. It also cuts the time needed to get credit verified.

The Federal Reserve System handles more than 18 million checks a day. That many checks, taped end to end, would reach from New York City to Billings, Montana.

In its second function, as the Government's bank, the Federal Reserve does two things: It keeps the Government's checking accounts; and it helps the Government handle its "IOU's."

When you pay taxes, your money doesn't necessarily go off to Washington. It probably goes to a local bank and winds up as a deposit in the Government's checking account at the nearest Federal Reserve Bank.

As the Government spends money—to buy arms and missiles, build dams, pay soldiers, or whatever—it writes checks on its accounts with the Federal Reserve, which keeps records and sends regular statements just as your bank does for you.

The Government has borrowed about $224 billion from the public. When the U.S. Treasury borrows, it gives the lenders an "IOU" in the form of a bond or other security. When you buy a U.S. Savings Bond, for example, you are lending money to the Government, and the "IOU" is that engraved piece of paper you get in exchange.

The Federal Reserve handles some of the paper work when the Government borrows. The securities are printed and the Federal Reserve issues them. It puts the money received for them into the Government's checking accounts.

The third function of the Federal Reserve involves supervising the member banks. The Federal Reserve issues regulations about what banks can or cannot do. It also examines banks and their records to see that they are being properly managed.

Each bank is examined at least once a year. It takes anywhere from a week to several months—depending on the size of the bank.

That brings us to the fourth—and perhaps most important—function of the Federal Reserve: managing the supply of money. This is where it becomes a factor in fighting inflation.

Regulating the money supply

Money, it is said, is like fire. Under control, both money and fire are very useful. Running wild, both can do great harm. It is the job of the Federal Reserve to keep money under control.

The Federal Reserve is not directly concerned with who gets money—or how money is spent. The free-enterprise system, with millions of people making their own decisions, determines such things.

The Federal Reserve deals in *totals* only. It tries to make sure the *total amount of money* and credit in the nation is about right—not too much, not too little—in relation to the supply of goods and services.

Too much money can make prices rise. That, we have already learned, is inflation. On the other hand, too little money can cause recessions and unemployment.

To prevent inflation or recession, the Federal Reserve System tries to keep the flow of spending in line with rising production and economic growth of the nation. Its aim is to try to maintain a high level of over-all business with reasonable stability in prices—and without interfering with people's freedom to use their money as they please.

There are three principal ways to get spending money: earn it, take it out of savings, or borrow it. The Federal Reserve works primarily through the medium of borrowed money.

Money for loans comes from two sources: first, from people who have saved and are willing to lend their savings; second, from commercial banks which have the power, within limits, to create "checkbook" money.

The Federal Reserve has scant influence over savings in general. But it can affect the amount of money that commercial banks can lend and thus, the amount of checkbook money they create.

When the prices of goods and services begin to rise, the Federal Reserve may decide to hold down on bank credit. This reduces spending with borrowed money—which helps bring total spending back in line with production of goods and services. Other things being equal, prices then should stop rising.

Conversely, when the country is in a recession and unemployment is rising, the Federal Reserve is likely to enable commercial banks to increase their lending. This stimulates spending with borrowed money and tends to increase production.

As production rises, unemployed workers can be called back to their jobs—and the factories begin to hum once more.

A balance of spending and production at high levels is what the Federal Reserve seeks. How does the Federal Reserve operate in seeking that balance?

There are three main tools which it uses to influence the supply of money.

First, it may make changes in the percentage of money which banks are required to maintain in reserve behind their deposits. If the percentage is 20 per cent, banks must have $1 in reserve for every $5 in deposits.

Now, let us suppose that the Federal Reserve wishes to stimulate the economy by putting more money into it. It could reduce the reserve requirement to 10 per cent. That would mean that the banks would have to hold only $1 for every $10 they received in deposits, and their lending capacity would be increased correspondingly.

Conversely, if the Federal Reserve increased the reserve requirement, it would limit the lending ability of the banks—and tend to reduce economic activity.

The second tool is the "discount rate"—the rate of interest which the Federal Reserve charges for loans to commercial banks.

If the Federal Reserve wishes to limit the growth in the money supply, it raises the discount rate. In turn, the banks raise the rate of interest they charge on mortgages, home loans and the like. This discourages borrowing and slows down the economy.

When a recession threatens, the Federal Reserve lowers the discount rate. This reduces the interest on bank loans and encourages borrowing, which stimulates the economy.

The third tool is keyed to the buying and selling of Government securities in the open market. A vast portfolio of these securities is held by the Federal Reserve. When it seems desirable to get a sluggish economy moving again, the Federal Reserve buys more Government securities. It draws a check to pay the seller. The check finds its way into a member bank's account. This increases the amount of reserves on deposit and enables the banking system in general to expand the amount of credit it can extend. Sale of Government securities by the Federal

Reserve, on the other hand, decreases the reserves of banks and reduces their lending power.

All these important activities of the Federal Reserve System, however, must fall within the framework of the broader economic policies of the Government. If the Government continues to spend far more than it takes in—because of a war, for example—the ability of the Federal Reserve to combat inflation is severely handicapped. Prices would then continue to mount and inflation would continue to run its course despite the activities of the Federal Reserve—as happened after the big buildup in Vietnam in mid-1965. The Federal Reserve soon tightened credit, but without help from a tax increase, inflation kept mounting.

Also, the Federal Reserve can do very little about demands of labor unions for excessively high wage increases and attempts by some companies to score exceptionally high profits.

"Guidelines" for wages and prices

The Government, however, has tried to enlist the co-operation of both labor and management in a program of voluntary restraint so as to prevent unwarranted increases in wages and prices.

This program, commonly called "guidelines" for wages and prices, had a degree of success between 1962 and 1965.

The "guideline" principle was based on this simple idea: Wage increases should not exceed increases in output per man-hour.

Thus, when the annual increase in the productivity of

labor averaged 3.2 per cent, average annual raises in wages were generally held at that level.

These "guidelines" broke down, however, in 1966. When productivity figures showed an average advance of 3.6 per cent, Administration advisers urged that the wage line be held at the 3.2 per cent figure.

The major labor unions balked at this. Their spokesmen said that "living costs" were moving up all the time. They claimed that profits had advanced sharply and they wanted a share. By means of strikes or threats of strikes, one major union after another broke the 3.2 per cent barrier. Wage costs of industry rose. Result: more upward pressure on prices.

It would seem, then, that the powers to check inflation are limited. The extent to which inflation can go depends, in the last analysis, on the amount of inflation the general public is prepared to take, on the size of the deficit it is willing to let the Government run because spending programs are not covered by taxes, and on people's resistance to specific products which are too highly priced as a result of excessively high wages and profits.

CHAPTER NINE

The Dollar on the World Stage

To most Americans, a dollar is simply a dollar—a paper note which can be exchanged for some food, some clothing, some housing, some medical attention or other goods or services they desire.

But to the rest of the world and to those Americans who engage in international trade, the dollar bill is more than that. It is used not only to buy American goods but also to exchange goods between countries.

When businessmen of a given country trade with one another, they conduct their business in the currency of that country. Thus in France, they deal with one another in francs; in Britain, in pounds; in Germany, in marks; in Japan, in yen; in Argentina, in pesos; in Russia, in rubles.

But what happens when the Frenchman wants to sell to or buy from the Englishman, the German, the Japanese or the American? And how is each of these men to conduct his trade with any of the others, and with businessmen in all the other countries of the world?

The rise of the U. S. dollar

To enable trade to flow easily, the countries of the world, including the Communist countries, have come to use two principal currencies: U.S. dollars and British pounds.

With the decline of the British Empire and the rise of the United States after World War II, we heard less of the pound and more of the dollar. When the dollar appeared to be as good as gold—the U.S. government guaranteeing to provide gold in exchange for any amount of dollars at the rate of one ounce for $35—the dollar emerged as the supreme currency of international trade.

The dollar, once a purely national currency like any other, became an international currency into which the values of all different foreign currencies and goods could readily be converted. Thus all the countries of the world, with their many different currencies, achieved a common language which all might speak for the purposes of international trade.

Not only businessmen spoke this relatively new language—the language of the American dollar—in buying from and selling to one another. Their governments, too, came to use the dollar—along with gold—for the purpose of balancing their books—the books which kept the record of trade and other transactions between the different countries.

Thus people everywhere acquired a growing interest in the dollar. And it is literally true that the dollar belongs not just to Americans but to people throughout the world.

That being the case, the fate of the dollar—its strength

or its weakness—is of as much interest to the Englishman, Frenchman, German, Swiss, Italian, Rumanian and Japanese as it is to the American. If the purchasing power— the value—of the dollar should fall, the loss is suffered not only by Americans but also by everyone else, of almost every nationality, who is holding dollars.

On Jan. 1, 1968, foreigners held $33 billion worth of claims, payable in dollars. At that time, the U.S. Treasury held only $12 billion worth of gold—not nearly enough to honor its commitment to exchange gold for all outstanding dollars if all foreigners holding dollars insisted on turning them in for gold.

This inability of the United States to redeem all outstanding dollars has tied foreigners still more closely to the American currency.

Since they hold so many dollars, foreigners feel they have a right to raise their voices in demanding that the United States uphold the value of its currency. Theoretically, if the purchasing power of the dollar should fall, say, 10 per cent, foreigners would stand to lose $3.3 billion of the $33 billion they held as of Jan. 1, 1968.

Many foreigners, of course, have sought protection against loss by holding only a limited amount of dollars in cash and in bank accounts. They converted some into gold and invested the rest in stocks and other securities which might rise in value with the wave of inflation.

Nevertheless, they insist on protection of the value of the dollar—not only because of the dollars they are holding, but also because they are interested in preserving the American currency as the most satisfactory means of conducting international trade at the present time.

Eventually, another international "language" may be devised. Plans already have been formulated for creating "paper gold" (called SDR's—for "special drawing rights" of the International Monetary Fund). But for some time to come, this is likely to be a secondary type of international money. The dollar is the only one, already established in the field, which can serve the present and the immediate future.

What foreigners want U. S. to do

Foreign traders and holders of American dollars make two basic demands on the United States:

1. They want the United States to slow down or to halt its inflation (because inflation is reducing the value of their dollars and threatens to make the dollar a fluctuating, unstable means of measuring the exchange of goods between countries).

2. They want the United States to balance its accounts with the rest of the world because, as a result of the imbalance, the United States has been putting out too many paper dollars at a time when it has only a limited ability to redeem them with gold and at a time when the dollar is losing purchasing power because of inflation within the United States. By doing so, they complain, Americans are taking advantage of the fact that their dollar has become an international currency; and Americans are "imposing" on foreigners when they insist that the "paper dollar" be taken on faith in unlimited quantities in the present circumstances.

Our balance of payments

American Government officials, bankers and businessmen have been convinced that they should not further
strain the faith of foreigners in the dollar—and they have
supported a program designed to correct an unhealthy
situation.

This involves correcting the American balance-of-pay-
ments position—which is a way of describing the relationship between the amount of money leaving the country
each year and the amount entering the country.

The balance is favorable when we take in more than
we spend abroad. It is unfavorable when we spend more
than we take in.

Not long ago, the United States enjoyed a favorable
balance between exports and imports. In 1964, for example, the United States bought (or imported) about
$19 billion worth of goods from the rest of the world and
sold (or exported) about $25 billion worth. Thus the
trade balance in favor of the United States was $6 billion.

There were other factors, however, which worked
against the American position. Our tourists, fanning out
across the globe in 1964, spent $3 billion for transporta-
tion, accommodations, services and souvenirs. The rest
of the world, on the other hand, spent only about $1.4
billion in the United States.

Another major dollar outlay in 1964 was the investment
by American business abroad of $6 billion. Overseas in-
vestment returned $5 billion in income to the United
States.

Among the heaviest outlays were those made by the
U.S. Government. In 1964, Washington spent about $3

BALANCE OF PAYMENTS DEFICIT

(Billions of Dollars)

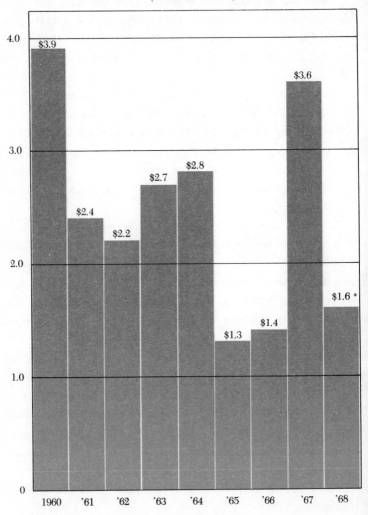

* Annual rate based on first half-year figures.

Source: U.S. Department of Commerce

billion to maintain American armed forces around the world. Then, there were American grants and loans, largely in the underdeveloped areas of the world. That bill came to $4 billion.

In the end, the big margin of American exports over imports was wiped out by Government spending, tourist spending and American investment abroad. The U.S. deficit for the year in the over-all balance of payments was $3 billion.

If this were an occasional problem, there would be little cause to worry. Unfortunately, the United States has had an unfavorable balance of payments for the greater part of the past 20 years.

Because of the excess of dollar expenditures over dollar receipts, foreigners found themselves holding more and more dollars. As the amount of their dollar holdings became increasingly greater than the amount of gold which the United States held in its coffers to redeem these outstanding dollars, foreigners became more and more nervous.

They began turning in their dollars for gold—until we had what became known early in 1968 as a "run" on the dollar and a "flight" to gold.

This raises the question of why gold should have such a powerful appeal to people of all nationalities in all parts of the world.

The real, intrinsic value of gold—independent of the value attached to it as an international currency—has yet to be established. Some believe that if gold were completely detached from money and if it were allowed to find its level simply as another metal, of use in dentistry,

THE OVERSEAS DEFICIT CAUSED
BY MILITARY EXPENDITURES

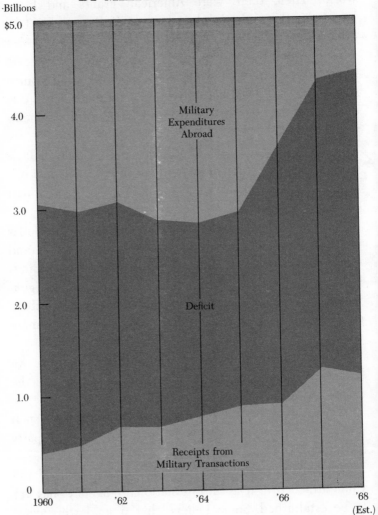

Billions

Military
Expenditures
Abroad

Deficit

Receipts from
Military Transactions

$5.0
4.0
3.0
2.0
1.0
0

1960   '62   '64   '66   '68
(Est.)

Source: U.S. Department of Commerce

industry and other commercial activity, its price would fall below the $35-per-ounce figure arbitrarily established by the United States and accepted by the other countries of the world. One London expert says gold valued only as a commodity would be worth but $8 an ounce.

But the fact is that it is difficult—perhaps impossible—to detach gold from money because millions of people all over the world have a strong emotional attachment to it as a property with the extraordinary power to resist whatever attacks are made upon it by time and by man. It is an attachment deeply rooted in history.

Gold over the years

The use of gold as money has been traced back to Abraham's time—about 1,900 years before the birth of Christ. Then, as now, it was relatively scarce, desirable and acceptable as payment for purchases and debts.

Gold coins, along with silver, were the principal monies of the civilized world for more than 3,500 years.

Over a period of time, changes were made in the hand-to-hand nature of money. People of wealth began depositing their gold with local goldsmiths for safekeeping. There were very few banks then, and the smith had facilities to protect considerable supplies of gold.

In those days, the smiths gave receipts—or chits—for gold deposits. Before long, the receipts themselves began to circulate as substitutes for the gold they represented. They were convenient and they were acceptable because they could be exchanged for gold any time the holder desired.

In some respects, this simple system was the forerunner

of the gold standard, which was used by many nations until the early 1930s. Under the gold coin standard, governments issued paper money which was backed by, and exchangeable for, gold. The amount of money circulating in a country was influenced by the amount of gold behind it: more gold, more money; less gold, less money. The system had several advantages.

Since governments couldn't increase the money supply without regard to their stock of gold, citizens were thought to be protected from inflation which invariably followed the printing of large supplies of new currency. The threat that the people would demand gold for their paper tended to keep politicians "honest."

The gold standard also was expected to keep a nation's payments to, and receipts from, foreign countries in rough balance. If a country on the gold standard bought more from, than it sold to, foreign powers over a prolonged period, a gold outflow would force a reduction in the amount of money circulating at home.

A smaller money supply, in turn, would tend to reduce the prices of things the country produced. Lower prices would make the country's goods and services more attractive to foreign buyers, stimulating exports, and would discourage purchases from abroad.

There were, however, some disadvantages to the gold standard. There was automatic and arbitrary restraint on the amount of money circulating within a country. This tended to curb prices and to put a damper on business activity, which in turn contributed to the problem of unemployment.

Another major drawback was the nature of gold itself.

The size of the gold supply always depended more on chance than need. The supply increased when discoveries of gold *happened* to be made—not when expanding world trade increased the *need* for money.

By the mid-1930s, major world powers were backing away from the gold standard. In 1933, the U.S. Government called in all gold coins and certificates and stopped redeeming paper money with gold at home.

Our paper money—no longer redeemable in gold—continued to circulate as freely as ever. And we came to believe that our monetary authorities, even without the rigid discipline of a gold standard, could avoid the pitfall of issuing too much money and thus destroying the purchasing power of the dollar. On the other hand, it was possible to increase the amount of money in circulation when necessary to combat unemployment.

Gold, then, became visible only as a commodity used in wedding rings, lockets, bracelets, wrist-watch bands and as fillings for teeth.

However, until recently gold served as a check on the amount of money which the U.S. Government could put into circulation. You recall that we have three principal types of money: coins, paper bills and bank deposits, which circulate as checks.

A law adopted by Congress forbade the Government to print more than $4 in currency for each $1 worth of gold it held in its possession. Since the Government's stock of gold was always limited, this put a ceiling on the amount of money the Government could issue, thereby giving the public some protection against abuse of the "printing presses."

This arrangement meant that the Government was obliged to hold a large supply of gold immobilized in the United States as a kind of "cover" or "security" for paper money in circulation. When foreign countries began to demand gold for their dollars, running down the U.S. Government's available supply of gold, the Treasury appealed for release of the immobilized stock so that it might have an additional amount available to meet foreign demands.

In March, 1968, the Congress lifted the gold "lid" on our currency supply. Technically, there now is no limit on the Government's use of the "printing presses" to turn out paper money, and the public must rely on the Federal Reserve money managers—rather than on the law—to limit the supply of money and credit.

At about the same time, the United States reached an agreement with friendly European countries whereby it no longer would sell gold abroad on the open market. The purpose was to help conserve the U.S. gold supply for use in settling accounts between governments while denying it to speculators on the open market who were gambling that gold would increase sharply in price.

The over-all aim was to gain additional time for the United States to put its house in order and to defeat French President Charles de Gaulle's aim to remove the dollar from its lofty position as the principal currency in foreign trade.

President de Gaulle regards the dollar as a symbol of American superiority. He would like the world to return to gold as its exclusive medium of international payments.

He began to worry Washington by demanding gold

in exchange for dollars held by France. He encouraged other countries holding American dollars to follow his example. His aim presumably was to run down the American stock of gold and to force the United States into "devaluation"—which would mean reducing the value of the dollar in relation to gold by raising the price of gold.

Changing the value of money

The world has had a recent example of "devaluation" in the case of Britain, which reduced the value of the pound by 14 per cent late in 1967. This meant that foreigners could buy a pound's worth of goods in Britain for $2.40—instead of $2.80, as before—a saving of 40 cents. It also meant that Britons, in buying goods abroad, would have to pay more than before because each of their pounds was worth 40 cents less.

In theory, this gave Britain an edge over its trading partners in the marketplace. Devaluation reduced the price of everything Britain sold to other nations. It raised the cost of everything Britain imported from abroad.

By this device, Britain hoped to expand exports and to reduce imports, thereby bringing its trade into balance and strengthening the nation's economy.

Other countries, however, react strongly against the use of this device. They feel it's "not cricket;" that it's an attempt by one country to take unfair advantage of others. And the latter often retaliate by devaluing their currency, too, so that they would all be back on an equal level.

In the case of the United States, which plays such a prominent role in world trade, the resentment would be all the greater if Washington were to devalue the dollar in relation to gold. It was regarded as virtually certain that other countries would devalue their respective currencies to the same degree, so as to deny the United States a trading advantage and to protect their share of the world market.

Thus, after all the upheaval, everyone would be back to where they were before, and nothing would be achieved. That, in itself, was a strong argument against President de Gaulle's design. And it explains why the other great trading countries of the world were anxious to cooperate with the United States and to help it restore the dollar to a position of strength, without recourse to such devices as devaluation.

Restoring the dollar to health

The prescription for reducing the rate of inflation in the United States called for deep cuts in federal spending and sharp increases in income taxes. This would reduce spending both on the part of the Government and on the part of the civilian population. With less money in the market competing for goods, economists believed that prices in time would no longer rise. The dollar would hold its value.

The prescription for correcting the balance of payments called for curtailing American dollar investments abroad, discouraging foreign travel (such travel would mean giving foreign countries more of our dollars), reducing dollar expenditures on American forces overseas and on foreign-aid programs, and expanding American exports.

These measures were closely interrelated. The chances of recovering a good trade surplus depended on keeping down the prices of our goods so that they would be more competitive in foreign markets. The crisis in our balance of payments was due in good measure to the fact that inflation was pricing our products out of foreign markets. The chances of stabilizing prices, then, would depend on measures to curb inflation.

There were bound to be loud outcries from those who would be affected by the proposed "austerity" and restrictive measures—those who felt the need to raise "Great Society" programs to a still higher level; to increase expenditures to relieve racial tensions by helping underprivileged Negroes; to uphold our military activities abroad and to continue helping underdeveloped countries in Asia, Africa, and Latin America.

The situation was one in which spending priorities had to be established; in which many would be hurt if austerity measures were adopted, and perhaps even more would be hurt if they were not.

CHAPTER TEN

Inflation in Other Countries

There is nothing new about inflation. It's as old as the use of money itself. Looking back, we see that our problems are hardly unique. And we can see how our inflation troubles compare with those of other countries.

Perhaps the earliest inflation on record took place in the year 3000 B.C. Egypt adopted a unit of money called the "skat."

The Government put so many skats in circulation to finance ambitious programs that the value of the currency went down and down. In the end it was worth nothing at all.

Alexander the Great touched off a wave of inflation in his part of the world when he increased the amount of money in circulation with the great store of gold and silver which he seized and brought home from Persia.

In Nero's time, the Romans debased the coinage so that money became virtually worthless. For a while, the Empire went back to bartering goods without using money.

How inflation ruined Germany

There was serious inflation in both Europe and Asia after the big wars of the twentieth century. The worst inflation of modern times was the one that hit Germany in 1923 and destroyed its currency—the mark. It provided a frightening example of what can happen if inflation is allowed to run unchecked.

The German mark, after the first World War, was worth about 19 cents. But in the 36 months leading up to December, 1923, German wholesale prices increased by a ratio of a *trillion* to one. To make that meaningful requires a translation into personal experience.

Consider the case of the college professor who drew an inflated salary of 10,000 marks a month, early in 1922. Two years before, his salary had been 2,000 marks a month—or the equivalent of $400.

The professor's 10,000 marks bought less in 1922 than his 2,000 marks had bought in 1920. By the summer of 1923, his salary had gone up to 10 *million* marks a month —and it bought him hardly anything at all.

Prices of goods were rising so fast, he could not get enough marks together soon enough to keep up. In desperation, the professor asked and received permission to draw his salary twice a month, then once a week, and finally twice a day.

Patrons in restaurants insisted on paying when served. If they didn't, the price of the meal often doubled while they were eating it.

A taxicab ride from a hotel in Berlin to the railroad station cost about 50,000 marks.

Beneficiaries seldom bothered to accept the proceeds

from life insurance policies. The settlement often was not worth the price of the stamp to claim it.

For the professor, the last straw came when he tried to pay the fare on a streetcar with a satchel full of inflated marks. It wasn't enough. Sadly, he emptied the marks into the street and walked home.

In the end, the German Government shut down its printing presses. Money had lost its meaning. All the mortgages in Germany in 1913—then worth about 10 billion U.S. dollars—could have been paid off in 1923 with one American penny.

Production came to a standstill. Germany was "broke".

How could this happen? Why were millions of Germans literally ruined, their life savings destroyed in the fire of inflation?

There are many explanations, but they come down to this:

The German economy was badly damaged by the first World War. The Government had difficulty in getting enough sound money and credit, either at home or from abroad, to meet its expenses in running the country. As a last resort, it turned on the printing press.

With goods of all kinds remaining scarce, the increasing amount of money printed by the Government kept sending prices up. As prices went higher, the Government and everyone else needed still more marks. As a result, the Government printed still more money. The race continued at a constantly increasing pace until it ended in collapse.

It is often said that Germany's "runaway inflation" played an important part in preparing the ground for the rise of Adolf Hitler. This points to the acute political as well as economic dangers which uncontrolled inflation can bring to a country—and to the entire world.

The inflation which wrecked what was left of the German economy after the first World War wiped out the middle class—white collar workers, teachers, and small businessmen. These were the people who provided a moderating influence on the nation's domestic and foreign policies. When they were destroyed by inflation, Germany developed two extremist camps—Nazi and Communist —and Hitler appeared on the scene to settle the issue, for the moment, in favor of his brand of totalitarianism.

Inflation after World War II

When World War II ended in 1945, much of the European continent again lay in ruins. But this time, after a period of severe hardship and monetary reforms by some of the European countries, the United States offered massive aid under the Marshall Plan. The aim was to prevent a repetition of what happened after World War I—to nurse the European countries back to economic and political stability and to avert the ravages of another runaway inflation.

By 1948, the tide began to turn. Homes, factories, offices—entire cities—were rebuilt. In a remarkably short time—considering the extent of the devastation—the countries of Western Europe were back on their feet, advancing toward new records of production.

Then came a new development—"creeping inflation," arising, in this case, from relative prosperity rather than from adversity. It bore a resemblance to what was happening in the United States.

Industrial workers, backed by influential trade unions, began pressing for higher wages—for a bigger slice of the growing national economic pie. Owners of the plants bid for higher profits. Governments, committed to "Great Society" programs of their own, sought a bigger share of the nation's output to meet the mounting bills for social welfare, education, defense and all the other expenditures involved in running a country.

One of the major elements in Western Europe's post-war inflation was the scarcity of labor. As European factories picked up steam, rapidly expanding the output of all kinds of consumer goods and industrial equipment both for domestic and foreign markets, more and more labor was required. By 1959, Western Europe, as a whole, reached "full employment."

While the demand for labor increased, the supply lagged behind. With the return of better times, more workers retired at an earlier age; fewer women would leave their homes for the factory; more youngsters remained in school until the age of 16, instead of leaving to start work at the age of 14, as many had done before. The number of working hours in the week was cut in most European countries. And the low birth rate indicated great difficulties in replenishing supplies of labor.

The more successful European countries sought to relieve the shortage of labor by importing workers from abroad—from Spain, Turkey, and Yugoslavia, for example. The supply, however, was still far short of demand. Employers competed against one another for the limited number of workers, sending the price of labor higher and higher.

INFLATION AROUND THE WORLD
Annual loss of currencies' buying power based on living costs

	1957-67	1966-67		1957-67	1966-67
	(Percent per year)			(Percent per year)	
Guatemala	.1	0	Norway	3.4	4.5
Venezuela	1.2	1.4/a	Mexico	3.5	3.2
Thailand	1.4	3.7	Italy	3.5	4.3
U.S.	1.8	3.5	Sweden	3.7	4.3
Luxembourg	1.8	2.5	Phillippines	4.0	5.5
Honduras	1.9	2.5	Denmark	4.3	7.8
Canada	2.0	3.4	Finland	4.4	5.4
Greece	2.0	1.7	Japan	4.4	3.8
Australia	2.1	3.3	France	4.6	2.8
Belgium	2.2	3.2	China (Taiwan)	4.6	3.8
Germany (Fed. Rep.)	2.3	1.6	Israel	5.0	1.6
South Africa	2.3	3.3	India	6.1	11.7
U.A.R. (Egypt)	2.5	1.2	Spain	6.7	5.7
Portugal	2.7	3.8	Bolivia	6.8	6.6
Switzerland	2.7	3.8	Turkey	7.7	12.0
United Kingdom	2.8	2.3	Peru	8.5	9.1
Austria	2.9	3.8	Korea	9.5	9.5
Ireland	3.0	3.0	Colombia	10.3	7.3
New Zealand	3.0	6.2	Vietnam	11.1	30.1
Ecuador	3.1	3.7	Chile	20.1	15.4
Iran	3.1	2.2	Argentina	24.8	22.1
Pakistan	3.2	5.9	Brazil	31.7	23.0
Netherlands	3.3	2.9			

/a Percent increase.
Source: Computed by Economic Unit of USN&WR from data of International
Monetary Fund.

In West Germany, France, and Switzerland, for example, wages increased on an average of about 7 per cent a year between 1963 and 1967. In Italy and Sweden, the figure was more than 9 per cent. In Belgium, the Netherlands, and Denmark, it was over 10 per cent. In Britain, it was just under 5 per cent.

Wages were now rising at a much faster rate than the productivity of labor. In most cases, they increased roughly twice as fast as productivity. The higher costs of producing goods were passed on to consumers; prices went up; inflation was underway in Western Europe.

Between 1963 and 1967, prices increased on the average of about 3 per cent a year in West Germany and France. They rose about 4 per cent a year in Britain, Italy, Switzerland, Belgium and Norway. They went up still more in the Netherlands and Sweden—over 5 per cent a year. The figure was over 6 per cent for Denmark.

These high rates of inflation compared with average annual price increases of little more than 2 per cent in the United States during this period.

How Germany licked inflation

The European countries, while pleased about their expanding economies, became worried about the rate of their rising prices. They knew that "creeping inflation" could easily develop into a gallop which could imperil both their prosperity and their political stability. One country after another began taking measures to check the advance of prices.

West Germany proved to be the most successful of all,

becoming something of a model for Western Europe and other countries troubled by "creeping inflation."

Government spending was curbed. Sharp restraints were placed on bank credits. This was bound to produce a slowdown in business activity, and the year 1967, in fact, turned out to be West Germany's first serious business setback in 20 years. Production fell. Investment by business in new plant and equipment also declined. As factories cut back production schedules, unemployment rose to the highest level in eight years.

Nevertheless, German workers co-operated with the Government's anti-inflation drive to a remarkable degree. They voluntarily accepted a scaling down of wage increases.

A top German economist explained: "The average German, particularly the worker, knows and fears the dangers of inflation. The disastrous results of the inflations that followed the two World Wars are not yet forgotten here."

The Germans risked a recession as the price of bringing inflation under control—and they won. After a setback which proved less severe than had been expected, business picked up again. Output and profits increased again. Unemployment declined.

The increase in the cost of living during 1968 was held to less than 1 per cent, and most of that was due to higher sales taxes rather than to higher prices for goods. The German Bundesbank, in its annual report, said:

"For the first time in eight years, the value of our money, in terms of consumer purchasing power, has ceased to decline."

Stable prices enabled West Germany to compete more

successfully in selling its products abroad, and the country achieved an exceptionally favorable trade balance by the end of 1968.

A Frankfurt banker, brimming with optimism, predicted:

"The business shake-out of 1967 cleared the road for a vigorous new upswing that is likely to last at least through 1969 and into 1970."

Other European countries similarly succeeded in reducing their rates of inflation by restricting bank credits, curtailing Government expenditures and increasing taxes. These measures had the effect of slowing down business activity, creating unemployment, holding down the rate of wage increases, and reducing purchases by the public.

Less efficient enterprises were eliminated by the intensified competition which developed. The more efficient ones produced goods which were able to compete more successfully in foreign markets, thereby helping to increase exports and to improve their country's trade balance.

For a period of twelve months between the summer of 1967 and the summer of 1968, Italy, as in the case of West Germany, held its rate of price increases to less than 1 per cent.

The Netherlands, Switzerland and Sweden cut back their rates of inflation to between 1 and 2 per cent. Belgium, Austria and Norway held their rates to between 2 and 3 per cent.

The troubles of Britain and France

In Britain, inflation increased to a high 5.3 per cent. In France, it rose to 4.6 per cent. These two countries had special difficulties.

Inflation in Britain must be considered in the light of what has happened to Britain since the end of World War II. When Britain lost much of its empire and much of the influence it formerly had among the members of the Commonwealth, it lost some of the special trade and other economic advantages which helped Britain become a major world power. Heavily dependent on foreign trade, it was obliged to compete more strenuously than ever before in trying to sell its industrial products abroad.

Competition from the United States, West European countries and Japan proved to be stiff. Rising prices in Britain, due in part to heavy government expenditures on social welfare programs and to increasing wages, had the effect of pricing British goods out of various markets.

In November, 1967, the British Government devalued the pound in an attempt to increase exports, discourage imports and thereby reduce the heavy deficit in Britain's balance of payments.

The danger of devaluation, as mentioned earlier, is that competitor countries might retaliate by resorting to the same device of cheapening the price of their currencies, and thereby of their goods being offered for sale abroad. In this respect, Britain was fortunate because its principal competitors refrained from retaliation.

Devaluation produced some of the effect which had been sought. Exports improved and so did the balance of payments. The pound, which had been slipping in value, became stronger. Money, which had been emigrating from London to other capitals considered to be safer, began flowing back to Britain.

As optimism returned, predictions were made that Britain would achieve a surplus of 500 million pounds in its 1969 balance of payments. But as the beginning of 1969 approached, the forecasters turned more conservative and cut this estimate by half.

Inflation continued to cloud Britain's future. Wildcat strikes pushed up the level of wages and the price of goods. Imports continued at a high level as consumers indulged themselves in heavy purchases of foreign products.

A troublesome question persisted: Can Britain sustain the burden of its Welfare State and meet the demands of its people for still higher living standards?

The answer, it seems, will depend on whether Britain can bring its inflation under better control and on whether it can hold down the price of its goods so that they might compete more successfully abroad. Such achievements, in turn, depend on a greater degree of efficiency and productivity than British labor and industry have displayed so far, in the opinion of European economists.

In France, President de Gaulle governed the nation's economy with a strong hand for a number of years. He was able to check the rate of inflation and to stabilize the value of the franc by keeping a tight rein on expansion of business activity. This had the effect of allowing unemployment to rise and thereby restraining the gains in workers' incomes.

The outcome of this policy was an explosion of strikes

in the summer of 1968 which, for a while, threatened to bring down the De Gaulle regime itself. The settlement, eventually negotiated, involved higher wages for workers. These, in turn, meant higher prices for French products and greater difficulty in competing against the lower-priced, more efficient manufactures of West Germany and Japan.

While wages were rising at the rate of about 13 per cent in 1968, the French Government embarked on a campaign to raise productivity so as to check inflation and to make the prices of French goods more attractive to foreign buyers.

It was feared that streamlining French enterprises would lead to a sharp increase in the number of unemployed. At the same time, the rising cost of living, caused in part by higher wages for workers, was likely to lead to fresh demands for another round of wage increases.

As in the case of Britain, there were troublesome questions about the ability of the French Government and people to deal with the problem of inflation.

Economists hold different views about inflation in advanced, industrialized countries and inflation in the less advanced, developing countries.

Some argue that there is no need or justification for serious inflation in the industrialized nations. They claim that monetary stability can be achieved if Governments balance their budgets, if caution is used in expanding credits through the banking system and if workers and employers exercise restraint in seeking higher wages and higher profits. The essential ingredient, according to this view, is responsibility on the part of the major elements which go into establishing the prices of our goods and services—Government, banks, workers and employers.

Many West European economists are particularly vigorous in their opposition to inflation. While admitting that it may stimulate business activity and contribute to full employment, in the long run, they say, inflation "distorts" a nation's economy (by expanding one area at the expense of another), upsets its trade balance and brings about a recession, accompanied by unemployment.

They tend to be critical of the United States for failing to act early enough and vigorously enough to check its rate of inflation. Whereas the rate of inflation was lower in the United States than in many West European countries during the earlier part of the 1960's, the situation was reversed in 1967 and 1968. For a 12-month period between the middle of 1967 and the middle of 1968, Germany, Italy, the Netherlands, Switzerland, Sweden, Belgium, Austria and Norway brought their rates of inflation down to less than 3 per cent. During the same period, prices in the United States increased more than 4 per cent.

European economists ask why the United States did not act the way these Western European countries did in order to hold down prices.

Many American economists share the critical views of their European colleagues. However, others point out that there is a great difference between the burdens carried by the United States and those borne by Western Europe. The high cost of conducting the war in Vietnam and the high cost of new social welfare programs are often cited to explain why the rate of inflation in the United States overtook that in various countries of Western Europe.

Some economists make two more points:

• Inflation is a price which countries must pay if they want "full employment."

• Inflation promotes economic growth.

These points are advanced very often to explain the exceptionally high rates of inflation in the less developed countries of the world.

Turmoil in South America

Some of the most extreme cases of inflation in recent years are to be found in South America. Between 1961 and 1966, the cost of living in Brazil increased each year by an average of 60 per cent. For Uruguay, the figure was 40 per cent; Argentina, 27 per cent; Chile, 27 per cent; Colombia, 15 per cent; Peru, 10 per cent.

These countries, with the exception of Uruguay, claim that they were increasing their output of goods and services during each of these inflationary years. The average increase for each person was 1.2 per cent in the case of Brazil; 1.1 per cent in the case of Argentina; 2.6 per cent in the case of Chile; 1.4 per cent in the case of Colombia, and 3.2 per cent in the case of Peru.

If we take a closer look at these figures, we find that Brazil, with the highest rate of inflation, had among the lowest rates of increase in output of goods and services. Peru, with the lowest rate of inflation, had the highest rate of growth.

This might suggest that there is more growth when there is less inflation. However, economists have not been able to establish a definite and clear relationship between inflation and economic growth. They can cite cases where there has been greater growth with higher rates of inflation, and cases where there has been hardly any growth at all in countries which have been free of inflation.

Juscelino Kubitschek, when President of Brazil, claimed he could not have built the new capital of Brasilia in the 1950's without resorting to a policy of inflation. However, his critics maintain this kind of inflationary development brought serious consequences.

The rate of inflation accelerated until it reached a peak of more than 80 per cent in 1963. It carried the country to the edge of widespread disorder. It also complicated Brazil's problems of balancing its trade and attracting foreign capital to help develop its resources.

Similar problems arose in the case of other South American countries troubled by rising rates of inflation. In general, it was agreed that growth, accompanied by little or controlled inflation, was far better than growth with increasing rates of inflation because runaway inflation eventually could destroy whatever growth had been achieved.

A new Government which took power in Brazil embarked on a policy of reducing the rate of inflation and stabilizing the country's currency. This meant reducing the swollen deficits of the Government by raising taxes, holding down the expansion of credit and curtailing increases in wages and salaries.

Measures of this kind, of course, were unpopular. There was a decline in production and employment.

The rate of inflation, however, was reduced to about 25 per cent in 1968. After taking the country through a

recession, the Government believed it had laid the ground-
work for a new advance on a healthier basis. Exports increased and investments flowed into Brazil at an increasing
rate.

However, the high rate of population growth continued
to complicate the per capita economic advance of the
Latin American countries as a whole. Widespread poverty
placed a heavy burden on their Governments. Demands
for more education and social welfare increased this burden and made it extremely difficult to avoid budgetary
deficits, especially when the armed forces insisted on
maintaining or increasing their share of the economic pie.

Dependence on individual products or raw materials—
such as copper in the case of Chile—made them vulnerable
to fluctuating prices which exports of these goods would
bring on foreign markets. When prices were high, the
situation might be relatively good. When they were low,
it might become painful. At the same time, prices of
manufactured goods which these less developed nations
had to import from the industralized countries might very
well be increasing.

To reduce their dependence on foreign manufactured
goods, a number of South American countries, notably
Argentina, Brazil and Chile, embarked on industrialization
programs at a rapid pace. They restricted or excluded
imports of foreign products and gave domestic producers
a free hand. The absence of foreign competition enabled
domestic producers to operate inefficiently while taking
extraordinarily high profits.

These and other factors, including resistance to higher

taxes by the wealthy and more powerful citizens, make the battle against inflation in Latin America a most difficult and uncertain one.

Inflation in Asia

The less developed nations of Asia similarly have difficulties in stabilizing their currencies, balancing their trade and developing their economies. Each country, as in Latin America, is a special case with its own particular problems.

South Vietnam and South Korea have had to contend with wartime situations which produce shortages of goods, sharply increasing amounts of currency and consequently inflation. In Malaysia, low prices for its tin and rubber had the effect of reducing its earnings from abroad and increasing the problem of balancing its trade.

The worst case of inflation occurred in Indonesia. When the Sukarno Government turned on the printing presses to cover its rising budgets and deficits, the increased supply of money in relation to the limited amount of goods touched off an inflationary spiral in the late 1950s. Higher prices led to demands for higher wages. These, in turn, led to still greater budgets, greater supplies of money and greater amounts of inflation.

Economists generally agree that inflation is self-generating. Once it gets underway, it becomes difficult to slow down and stop. Even after the Sukarno regime was overthrown, the momentum which had already been built up carried Indonesia's rate of inflation to new heights. For the 12-month period ending in July, 1966, the rate reached 1,500 per cent.

As in Brazil, a new government undertook the task of

bringing order out of the monetary chaos which had developed in Indonesia. Controls were put into effect to hold down the supply of money and credit. The machinery to collect taxes was tightened. Special inducements were offered to attract foreign capital so as to revive and to expand the nation's output of raw materials and manufactured goods. These and other measures brought the rate of inflation down to 112 per cent for the calendar year 1967. The rate was cut still more—to about 60 per cent—during 1968.

Whereas West Germany has emerged as the example in Europe of prosperity through balanced economic growth and relatively stable currency, Japan has become the counterpart example in Asia. Japan held its rate of inflation to less than 6 per cent during 1968 while increasing its output of goods and services an estimated 10 per cent. The Japanese Government's Economic Planning Agency predicted that the country's total output in 1985 will be 4 times greater than it was in 1968.

The successes of these two countries have earned the respect of economists and others both in the developed and in the developing countries of the world.

West Germany had demonstrated to industrialized countries of the West how restraint on the part of Government, banks, workers and employers can reduce a nation's rate of inflation and set the stage for more satisfactory economic progress.

Japan had demonstrated to both industrialized and developing countries how a nation could emerge from feudalism and from a devastating defeat in war to become one of the most productive states in the world.

One of the factors of success in the case of most industrialized countries is their ability to expand productivity.

Raymond F. Mikesell, economics professor at the University of Oregon, pointed out during testimony before the Senate Subcommittee on American Republics Affairs in 1968 that "half to two-thirds of the annual growth in real output in the United States and in the industrially advanced countries of Europe has been accounted for by increases in productivity as contrasted with increases in labor and capital inputs—that is, productivity as against increases in the amount of labor and capital and other resources applied to the production process."

He added: "A recent study of productivity growth in five major Latin American countries—Argentina, Brazil, Chile, Colombia, and Mexico—shows that, except possibly for Mexico, productivity growth has contributed little or nothing to the growth of output in these countries during the post-war period."

His conclusion was that inflation, together with governmental policies associated with it, was responsible to a high degree for the low productivity of South American countries, their excessive self-sufficiency and their chronic shortages of foreign exchange for the purchase of foreign goods.

Some Latin American economists argue that it is the low productivity, together with other factors, which produces the inflation, rather than the other way around. Both cases may be true. Low productivity may contribute to inflation, and inflation may contribute to low productivity.

It seems clear, however, that increasing productivity

and relatively stable currencies are important ingredients for economic progress both in the industrialized and the developing nations. As indicated earlier, these call for restraint on the part of the principal factors which account for our prices. Unfortunately, there often is a great shortage of such restraint.

CHAPTER ELEVEN

Looking Ahead

Is inflation inevitable?

Is there no way of stabilizing the value of our money so that a dollar is worth a dollar—so that many people might be spared the hardship and deception caused by inflation?

In the years ahead, what's likely to happen to our dollar? to prices? to our world trade position? to our standard of living?

We might consider these questions in this concluding chapter. In doing so we can review some of the key points to keep in mind about inflation and your dollar.

If we examine the matter, we discover that there are two different types of inflation. We might call one "accidental" and the other "deliberate."

"Accidental" inflation

"Accidental" inflation is the result of demands by Government, business and labor for a bigger slice of the

economic pie. As a result of these demands—in a country
dedicated to full employment and Government-guaranteed
prosperity—we get a situation where there is more money
in circulation than there are goods which can be bought
with it. Hence the saying: too much money chasing too
few goods. The net result is rising prices—and inflation.

Neither the Government, when it resorted to inflationary
"deficit financing," nor the labor unions, when they
exacted higher wages in new contracts, nor corporations,
when they took higher profits, intended to produce inflation as a result of their actions. In fact, all would hope
that nothing of the kind would occur. Yet inflation, while
unintended and "accidental" as far as Government, labor
and business are concerned, was the natural consequence
of their actions.

Take the case of the Government in time of war, which
affords the best example of what happens. The Government's requirements are then so enormous that, taken
together with the continuing needs of the civilian population, the demand for goods of all kinds becomes many
times greater than the supply available to meet it.

Even so, the natural impulse toward price inflation
would be curbed if the Government paid for all its purchases with increased income from higher taxes on the
population. But the Government, even in time of war,
invariably evades the distasteful job of telling the people
the full price of the war bill, and asking them to pay it.
Instead, it asks the people to pay only part of the bill in
taxes; and it gets the rest through inflation.

This is done by establishing accounts in commercial
banks and issuing checks amounting to billions of dollars

to pay for all the things the Government could not buy with the inadequate amount of money secured from taxes and savings. The result of putting all these bank checks into circulation—the modern equivalent of the old-fashioned Government "printing press"—is to expand the nation's money supply. Wage and price controls—as in World War II and Korea—tend to suppress inflation for a time, but when controls are removed, inflation breaks out.

· The Treasury's budget deficit for the fiscal year ending June 30, 1968, came to $25.4 billion—the highest since World War II. This excess of Government spending over income was translated into increased indebtedness and inflated currency.

The national debt now exceeds $350 billion and the interest charges on that debt come to about $15 billion a year—another increasing burden on the taxpayer.

The total money supply at the end of 1967 (the total amount of currency in circulation and money in checking accounts) reached $181 billion—an increase of $11 billion over the previous year. This represents an increase of more than 6 per cent—or about double the normal 3 per cent annual increase considered justified by the growth of the nation's economy. And within this figure lies the "printing press" money issued by the Government in the form of its bank checks.

These provided the additional money which fed the price spiral. The greater amount of money, in short, enabled Government and consumers to bid up the prices for the limited supply of goods in the market. The result, of course, was constantly higher prices—that is, inflation.

This happened during the Revolutionary War; during the War of 1812, when prices increased 25 per cent; during the Civil War, when they shot up 75 per cent; during World War I, when they doubled; during and after World War II, when they went up 70 per cent; during the Korean War, when they increased 12 per cent; and during the Vietnam War (to 1968), when they rose again by 12 per cent.

The Government, in each instance, did not issue the additional money for the purpose of inflating the currency. Its aim, of course, was simply to pay its bills. However, the way it went about getting this money—issuing checks in order to appropriate a bigger slice of the nation's output—had the effect of expanding the total money supply in an unhealthy manner and of inflating prices. As a result, what the consumer was spared in direct taxes he lost in the higher prices he had to pay for goods and services.

One of the advantages to the White House in resorting to "hidden taxes" of this kind is that it may divert the anger of consumers from the Government to the stores, which unhappily appear to be responsible for the increased prices. In time, of course, people learn what has taken place; but by then, the Government in power may have left office, and its members would not be too concerned about what the public had belatedly discovered.

However, just as the evil that men do lives after them, so do the consequences of the spending practices of government during and between wars. The dollar which we earn and spend today bears all the scars and all the anemia inflicted on it by one Administration after another throughout American history.

Prices today are 2½ times as high as they were before World War II; 4½ times as high as in 1900. And the dollar is correspondingly poorer in purchasing power.

A New York restaurant created a sensation when it celebrated its 100th anniversary by charging 1868 prices for a dinner based on its original 1868 menu. The price for the five-course dinner was 12 cents. It consisted of soup, 2 cents; sausage, 4 cents; liver with salad and potatoes, 3 cents; pie, 2 cents, and coffee, 1 cent.

That, as some might nostalgically say today, was when a dollar was a dollar, and a cent was a cent. It's only fair to add, however, that a dollar was hard to come by in "the good old days."

Government, while it is the principal actor in the continual assault on the value of the dollar, cannot be blamed exclusively for all the damage. Labor unions and large corporations also played a role.

Between 1960 and 1964, wages in the United States increased about 3 per cent annually. That rate of increase, according to some economists, was justified by an increase in output per worker—and therefore did not have an inflationary effect on prices. By 1967, however, labor unions were insisting upon, and were securing, annual wage increases of 5 per cent, while the increase in output per man hour came to only 1 per cent. And the result was wage inflation. The next year, 1968, contracts in the steel and aerospace industries sent labor costs up more than 6 per cent.

The high wages which organized labor was able to command tended to work against the anti-inflationary program of the Government. And while the Government was trying to cut down on spending, on the one hand, labor unions were trying to increase it, or at least to maintain it, on the other. The result was continued inflation—and less satisfactory results from the anti-inflationary "medicine" than would otherwise have been the case.

The labor unions could make out a case for their increased demands. They were able to argue that rising prices and increased taxes were reducing the "take-home" pay of their members—and therefore were reducing their standard of living.

Statistics supported their arguments. Though pay increases were record-breaking, the average worker's buying power in 1968 was 21 cents a week less than it was in 1966.

Organized American labor, in short, was not willing to take a cut in "take-home" pay. Through the power of their unions, they insisted on passing on to their employers the increased tax enacted by Government and the increased cost of living brought about by higher prices.

Employers, in turn, passed these and other increased costs on to the purchasers of their products. In addition, they passed on the cost of a higher rate of profit to which they felt entitled by the declining purchasing power of the dollar.

In short, workers and their employers, seeking to defend their wages and their profits, saw no reason why they should bear the burden of still higher taxes and inflation. Therefore they shifted it to the consumer in the form of higher prices for steel, automobiles, refrigerators and all the other goods they produced. The result was to

SO YOU GET A PAY BOOST—
WHAT WILL BE LEFT?

Examples: Three families, each with four members, getting pay raises of 6 percent in 1968. Figures show that a raise of this size is almost wiped out by higher federal taxes, including the income surtax, an increase in the Social Security tax base, and a rise of 3 to 4 percent in living costs.

No. 1

Factory worker receiving $5,000 a year

Pay raise: $300

Federal income tax on
$300 raise . . . . $ 48
Increase in income tax . . . . $ 34
Higher Social Security tax . . . $ 13
Higher cost of living $150
    Total offset to pay raise . . $245

**LEAVING, OUT OF
A $300 RAISE: $55**

NO. 2

Construction worker
earning $8,000 a year

Pay raise: $480

Federal income tax on
$480 raise . . . . $ 82
Increase in income tax . . . . $ 85
Higher Social Security tax . . . $ 53
Higher cost of living $230
    Total offset to pay raise . . $450

**LEAVING, OUT OF
A $480 RAISE: $30**

NO. 3

Junior executive with
pay of $15,000 a year

Pay raise: $900

Federal income tax on
$900 raise $178
Increase in income tax $224
Higher Social Security tax . . . $ 53
Higher cost of living $418
    Total offset to pay raise . . $873

**LEAVING, OUT OF
A $900 RAISE: $27**

Note: State and local taxes, on the rise all over the U.S., will eat even deeper into any pay raises for millions of wage earners. Many workers, as a result, will find that wage boosts lag behind the increases in living costs and taxes.

sustain inflation and to weaken the effect of Government measures to curb it.

The Government, as an employer, could hardly point a finger of blame at other employers or at the unions. In the 10-year period ending in 1967, Post Office salaries were increased 56 per cent, while productivity improved only 2.5 per cent. During this same period, average wages in U.S. industry increased 44 per cent, with productivity going up 34 per cent.

And the Government, too, shifted part of the cost of its increased labor bill to the public. It raised the price of sending a letter or a package through the mails.

However, the ability of labor unions and employers to keep pushing up wages and prices is limited. The Government and the Federal Reserve System, acting together, can alter the general economic climate by holding down the nation's supply of money and credit.

Then there would be less money available for buying goods. Employers could not sell their products so easily. As sales dropped, their stocks would increase, and they would find it necessary to cut down production, and to lay off some of their workers.

The growing ranks of unemployed workers, with less money in their pockets, would add to the decline in sales. We would have a situation where employers would have to compete in selling their goods, and workers would have to compete in selling their labor. The result would likely be a decline in the prices of both goods and labor—or at least a strong curb against an increase in these prices.

These bear all the earmarks of a recession—and this is the kind of situation we had in 1958 and in 1960-61.

Unemployment increased to about 7 per cent of the civilian labor force. There was considerable idle plant capacity.

Prices of goods held firm, and even increased slightly, indicating the strength that unions have in upholding the price of labor even in times of adversity. But if the recession had continued and if the size of the unemployed army had grown still more, the impact on prices of both goods and labor would have been irresistible.

This brings us to a new phase of the inflation story—and to the second type of inflation we mentioned earlier—the "deliberate" as distinct from the "accidental" kind.

"Deliberate" inflation

Unemployment, as we know, creates unrest. The more unemployment there is, the more unrest. Thus a social-political factor is introduced into an economic problem. There is a limit to the amount of social unrest which a Government—any Government—can absorb. Hence there is a limit to the amount of unemployment which a Government can tolerate.

If necessary, Government will create jobs to reduce the number of unemployed. That's what President Franklin D. Roosevelt did at the time of the great depression in the 1930s. Concern over this problem led eventually to adoption of the Employment Act in 1946. Since then, by Act of Congress, the Government of the United States has been charged with maintaining maximum employment, production and purchasing power.

There is a limit, then, to the amount of unemployment which the Government can allow while correcting price inflation. The exact amount has never been definitely established, but economists, politicians and Government officials usually put it a few points above 4 per cent of the labor force. Four per cent unemployment is considered to be pretty close to "full employment"—though many "new economists" would prefer to see the jobless rate drop to 3.5 per cent.

When the unemployment figure therefore goes very far beyond 4 per cent, alarm bells start going off. Protests rise from the ranks of labor. Complaints are voiced by some politicians. Warnings are sounded by some economists. Businessmen and bankers, also concerned about the recession, join the chorus in demanding corrective action.

The "corrective action" they demand is a loosening of credit and an increase in the money supply. To halt the downturn and to start the upturn, the Federal Reserve System is persuaded (either by itself or by others) to make the borrowing of money easier. Accordingly, the rate of interest falls, businessmen are tempted to start new or to expand old operations, consumers find loans easier to get so they spend more on the good things of life, and things begin huming again.

The Government, for its part, may cut the tax rate so that people will have more money to spend, and it may increase its own budget deficits so as to add further inflation stimulants.

The result of these dual monetary measures by the Federal Reserve and fiscal measures by the Government is to end the economic downturn and to initiate an economic upturn. The end of the recession and the trend to a new boom or boomlet usually are accompanied by

an end to stable prices and the start of a fresh round
of rising prices--or inflation.

All of this, it will be recalled, was the result of deliberate moves by the Government and the Federal Reserve
Board to increase the total money supply. In other words,
it was the result of a deliberate policy of inflation.

It is now apparent that "deliberate" inflation is an
instrument used by the Government and the Federal
Reserve to end a recession and to stimulate an economic
revival.

The history of our economy is the history of these ups
and downs and these perpetual cycles—a boom, with
rising prices, followed by a downturn or recession, with
stabilized prices; then another boom, followed by another
downturn, and so on.

The course of inflation

This brings us to the question raised at the outset of
this chapter: Is inflation inevitable over the long haul?

We already have the elements of the answer.

In the case of what we have called "deliberate" inflation, the Government and the Federal Reserve hold an
instrument which they may or may not use, as they see
fit. But in view of the fact that Government cannot
tolerate an unreasonable amount of unemployment and
recession—under the mandate set by Congress in the
Employment Act—it is safe to assume that "deliberate"
inflation will continue to be used in the future, as it has
been in the past.

In the case of "accidental" inflation, so long as Governments resort to large-scale "deficit financing" to pay for

extraordinary costs (such as are involved in waging war or in undertaking vast social-reform projects), inflation is inevitable. It is inevitable because, as previously explained, the Government, instead of increasing taxes or borrowing savings to meet the full amount of the bill, resorts to a "hidden" or indirect tax. This tax takes the form of inflated currency which draws off part of the savings and earnings of the people through higher prices they are obliged to pay for everything they buy.

The tendency of Governments, particularly in time of war, is to resort to inflation to help pay for the swollen costs. We have been in a state of war, hot or cold, since World War II, and the chances are that we will continue to expend huge sums on war and defense for some time to come. In addition, huge sums are to be spent in the war against poverty on the home front. Taken together, these factors suggest expenditures of such mountainous proportions that Washington, for years to come, will continue to be tempted into "deficit financing" and inflation as the easiest way out of a painful financial situation.

As for "accidental" inflation caused by rising wages and profits:

So long as it is national policy to maintain a full measure of employment, production and purchasing power, economists feel that inflation pressures will persist. This becomes inevitable because full employment establishes a "seller's market" for labor. It enables workers to exact a higher price for their labor than is justified by their output, and it permits less productive marginal labor to come into the market at a high cost.

Manufacturers pass on to the public the higher labor

costs in the form of higher prices for their goods, and the inflationary infection eventually spreads through the entire economy. Higher prices, in turn, produce demands for still higher wages and higher profits, and we are swept into a wage-price spiral.

Thus we cannot expect to have full employment and price stability at the same time. No modern industrial nation anywhere has been able to do it for very long. If we are to have full employment, we must pay the price in inflation. If we are to have relative price stability, we must pay the price in some unemployment.

Economists have drawn up tables showing different degrees of price stability resulting from different rates of unemployment: as unemployment goes down, prices go up; as unemployment goes up, prices go down. One economist suggests that an unemployment rate of 8 per cent of the total working population would be required to achieve absolute price stability—that is, to halt any increase in prices. If the rate of unemployment fell to 4 per cent, then the annual increase in prices (the rate of inflation) would be 3 per cent. If unemployment were to fall still more to 2 per cent, then the rate of inflation would rise to 6 per cent.

An unemployment rate of 8 per cent is generally considered today to be totally unacceptable in this country. That being the case, we may conclude that absolute price stability is virtually impossible. On the other hand, a 6 per cent rate of inflation in order to reduce the rate of unemployment to 2 per cent is equally unacceptable. Just as one would produce an outburst from the swollen army of unemployed, the other would produce an outburst from housewives and other consumers protesting against the runaway rise in prices.

What we are likely to have in the future is what we have been getting in the past—a relationship fluctuating somewhere between the two extremes. In other words, as the rate of inflation fluctuates between 1 per cent and 4 per cent, the rate of unemployment will vary from 6 per cent to 3 per cent. These are amounts of inflation and unemployment with which consumers and workers evidently feel they can live.

The question sometimes is asked why we should not allow inflation to run freely since it appears to bring prosperity, full production and more jobs than there are workers.

The answer, of course, is that a limited amount of inflation may be a good thing in halting a recession and in stimulating the economy. Runaway inflation, however, would eventually turn a "boom" into a "bust." The feverish chase by too much money for too few goods would send prices soaring and would send the value of the dollar plummeting. Deteriorating value of money would lead to reckless investment and wild speculation in stocks. The economy would become distorted, unbalanced.

In time, prices would reach such heights that some consumers would be unable to keep up and they would stop buying. Manufacturers would find themselves stuck with goods they could not sell. Investors, belatedly recognizing that prices of stocks had become divorced from reality, would begin to unload their securities. And the collapse, with varying degrees of panic, would be under way.

There is another important reason why the Government tries to hold inflation—and the value of the dollar—within manageable limits. We pointed out in a preceding chapter that the dollar no longer is purely an American currency. It is also held by nationals of most countries of the world since they began using it as a principal currency for conducting international trade.

This being the case, if the dollar falls in value, foreigners holding it are unable to buy as much with it as before. A sharp fall in the value of the dollar could cause a panic abroad and disrupt the use of the dollar in international trade. The consequences could easily be economic turmoil throughout a large part of the world which could trigger a world-wide crash.

It is therefore clear that the United States has assumed an international responsibility for the value of the dollar.

There is still another, related aspect. We must export in order to pay for the goods we import, and to pay for our expenditures abroad, including those for our armed forces. To be able to export, our goods must be able to compete in price against foreign products. If our prices keep going up under the impact of inflation, we are unable to compete and unable to sell our goods abroad. A limit to inflation is therefore essential if we are to earn our way in the world.

The outlook for the dollar

What's likely to happen to the value of our dollar in the years ahead?

We have indicated that the dollar is almost certain to continue on the downward path which it has been

following during this century. The outlook, say economists, is for long-pull inflation—interrupted now and then
by periods of over-all price stability. The amount and
the speed of the dollar's decline will depend on the rate
and the frequency of inflation. These in turn would be
influenced by the Government's need of vast sums of
money—sums in excess of the maximum amount it feels
it can raise through taxes.

This need most likely will continue to be great. The
end of the Vietnam War should lift a heavy burden from
the budget and make it easier to meet the cost of domestic
programs for our cities, poverty and the like. But defense
costs will continue to be high in the absence of any genu-
ine understanding with Russia. It's questionable whether
we will reach such an understanding in our lifetime. And
there are many projects waiting in the wings to snap up
whatever billions of dollars are released by the end of
the Vietnam War—deferred space programs, for example.

Together with, or apart from, the Government's role
in causing inflation, we have the constant upward pressure on prices caused by the constant increase in wages
which labor unions are able to secure through their
monopoly bargaining power. These factors, too, are almost
certain to be present for an indefinite period.

On the other hand, we now know how to limit inflation,
to keep it from galloping and bringing on a major crash,
such as the one of 1929. This is done by regulating the
nation's money supply. We already have identified the
dual instruments for doing this—the credit-control powers
of the Federal Reserve System and the fiscal powers (tax-
ation and spending) of the Federal Government.

The Government—whatever party is in power—can be relied upon to use this instrument to hold inflation within acceptable limits. We indicated that these limits lie somewhere between 1 per cent and 4 per cent as an annual increase in the nation's consumer price level.

A "conservative" Government might be expected to accept an inflation of about 1 per cent or 2 per cent as its target. That would hold prices within manageable limits. However, the consequences, as pointed out earlier, might be a somewhat higher rate of unemployment. One of the major problems faced at the outset of the Nixon Administration was how to bring down the rate of inflation without increasing the rate of unemployment.

A "liberal" Administration might be more disposed toward keeping unemployment down to a rock-bottom minimum—at the cost of letting inflation run 3 per cent or perhaps a bit more.

That amount of inflation, however, becomes quite disturbing if allowed to run for any length of time. And the chances are that even a "liberal" Administration would not want to let inflation exceed 3 per cent for very long without taking corrective measures.

All things being equal, and barring national and international emergencies, these are the rates of inflation we may expect in the years ahead. The prices of American goods should be able to compete satisfactorily in foreign markets because comparable or even higher rates of inflation are likely to be in progress in other countries. American exports should be able to recover some of their lost ground. The dollar should recover its strength, both at home and abroad.

Persistent inflation, even on a reduced scale, will nevertheless have a cumulative impact and will transform prices so as to appear shocking and hardly recognizable from where we stand today.

If prices should increase on an average of 3 per cent a year, they will double every 24 years. If they increase on an average of 2 per cent a year, they will double in 35 years—and the value of a dollar of 100 cents would fall to 50 cents.

Assuming a 2 per cent increase, continuing the pattern of the past, prices, on the average, will be double what they are today by the turn of the century.

Some prices, of course, will rise more than others. A day in the hospital, which in many areas now costs $75 for a semiprivate room, will be $630 by the year 2000, if past trends continue. The price of a weekly foodbasket for a family of four, now $40, will be $112; a man's suit, now $80, will be $270; a $2 haircut will climb to $10; a new car, now $4,000, will be $9,900, and a year in college, now $2,570, will require $6,000.

Rents, according to these projections, will double. So will the price of a house. If your house is worth $30,000 today, it should bring about $60,000 by the year 2000. A $40,000 house will rise to $80,000; a $50,000 house to $100,000 and so forth.

The majority of Americans can be expected not only to ride the inflation wave successfully but also to raise their standard of living each year as the country continues to increase its annual output at a rate of about 4 per cent a year in real terms.

Thus the median income of a typical American family,

WHAT INFLATION MAY BRING

DAY IN HOSPITAL

Cost now: $75,
in semi-private room
Year 2000: $630

NEW CAR

Price now: $4,000
Year 2000: $9,900

MAN'S HAIRCUT

Price now: $2
Year 2000: $10

MAN'S SUIT

Price now: $80
Year 2000: $270

FOOD FOR FOUR

Price now:
$40 per week
Year 2000: $112

A YEAR IN COLLEGE

Cost now: $2,570
at private school
Year 2000: $6,000

HOUSE

Price now: $40,000
Year 2000: $86,000

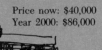

HAVING A BABY

Cost now: $200
for obstetrical care
Year 2000: $640

BUT—INCOMES WILL BE UP, TOO.

A typical family with income now of **$8,000** a year may have an annual income of **$36,000** by the end of this century, if recent trends continue.

Note: Today's prices, in the examples above, are typical current prices. Year-2000 prices are projections by the Economic unit of USN&WR, based on past trends.

now at $8,017 a year, will increase to about $36,000 by the turn of the century—more than four times the present amount. Allowing for the increased cost of living (inflation) and increased taxes, it is estimated that the buying power of this family will still be double what it is today.

Where inflation strikes with cruelty is in its impact on the older members of the community. Their fixed pensions and incomes are relentlessly eroded as the purchasing power of each dollar falls year after year. The value of savings of all people—young and old—is also threatened with constant erosion unless they have some understanding of how to protect their interests.

There are no guarantees of success. No one has yet devised a foolproof method of keeping ahead of inflation.

The best solution, of course, would be to prevent inflation in the first place. But the chances of that happening are very slim. The record of the past provides some guidance to the future. Prices went up in 49 of the last 68 years—or about in 3 of every 4 years. They stayed the same in only 6 years, and they declined in only 13 years—or about 1 year of every 5.

The conclusion is quite clear: We are living in an "age of inflation." Knowledge of the nature of inflation, therefore, becomes more and more important for those who seek to keep up with an inflationary world.

Glossary of Words and Phrases
Related to Inflation

APPRECIATION—An increase in the market value of an asset.

ARBITRATION—The settlement of disputes between labor and management by a third party.

ASSET—A property or a right that has value, such as stocks, bonds, real estate, and so forth.

AUSTERITY PROGRAM—A government program which involves high taxes and/or controls over production which serve to cut the level of consumption.

BALANCE OF PAYMENTS—The record of a country's total payments to and receipts from foreigners.

✳ BALANCE OF PAYMENT DEFICIT—A situation where the amount of money leaving a country is greater than the amount entering it, the difference made up in gold sales or some type of credit.

BEAR MARKET—A market in which prices of most stocks are declining.

BLUE CHIP STOCK—The common stock of a large corporation with a well-established record of earnings and dividends.

BOND—A form of loan to a corporation or government. The issuer promises to repay the purchaser at a fixed rate over a fixed period of time.

BOOM-BUST—A cycle involving first a rapid expansion of business activity, followed by a drop in activity to a low level. The end result is unemployment, low incomes, shrinking profits and low prices.

BUDGET DEFICIT—The result when expenditures exceed revenues.

BUDGET SURPLUS—The result when revenues exceed expenditures.

BULL MARKET—A market in which prices of most stocks are rising.

BUYER'S MARKET—A market in which buyers have an advantage because supply has exceeded demand and prices have come down.

CAPACITY—The peak at which a firm or industry can produce while operating on a normal schedule and utilizing all its plant and equipment.

CAPITAL—All monies and goods used in the production of other goods, including plants and machinery. It supplements land and labor as the third of three major factors of production.

CAPITAL EXPENDITURE—The money spent for a fixed asset, such as a business or piece of machinery.

CAPITAL GOODS—Goods employed to produce other goods.

CASH—"Legal tender," such as coins and paper money.

CHECKBOOK MONEY—Checks drawn from individual checking accounts and circulating as money. They now account for the bulk of the total amount of money in circulation.

COLLATERAL—Property pledged to secure a loan.

COLLECTIVE BARGAINING—Negotiations between representatives of industry and of labor to arrive at mutually agreeable terms governing the conditions of employment.

COMMON STOCK—The capital stock of a corporation, giving the holder an ownership interest in the corporation's earnings and assets after prior claims have been met.

CONSUMER PRICE INDEX—A monthly measure of changes in the retail prices of goods and services as compiled by the Bureau of Labor Statistics.

COST-PUSH INFLATION—A type of inflation in which rising costs push prices up.

CREEPING INFLATION—A gradual but steady increase in the cost of goods and services.

CREDIT—An exchange of goods or services for a promise of later payment.

CREDIT CONTROL—The practice of regulating the flow of new credit into the economy.

CURRENCY—The circulating portion of a nation's money supply.

DEFICIT FINANCING—The practice by the Government of spending more money than it receives in revenue and taxes.

DEFLATION—A fall in price level usually following a drop in the supply of money and credit, and/or a sharp cutback in consumer spending.

DEMAND DEPOSIT—A bank deposit or a checking account which may be drawn on without prior notice to the bank.

DEMAND-PULL INFLATION—A type of inflation in which scarcity of goods and strong demand combine to bring about a rise in prices.

DEPRECIATION—A drop in the value of fixed assets.

DEPRESSION—A long period in which business activity is sluggish and in which pessimism marks the attitudes of businessmen and consumers.

DEVALUATION—A reduction in the value of a country's currency in relation either to gold or to another currency.

DISCRETIONARY INCOME—That part of an individual's income from which postponable purchases may be made—or which may be set aside as savings.

DISPOSABLE INCOME—That part of an individual's income after deductions for all types of taxes and government fees.

EASY MONEY—A term which describes a condition of low interest rates and great availability of credit.

ECONOMIC GROWTH—An increase in the capacity to produce goods and services along with a corresponding increase in the production of those goods and services.

FACE VALUE OF AN INSURANCE POLICY—The amount of money paid as a death benefit.

FEDERAL RESERVE BANK—The Government-chartered bank which has the power to influence other banks and to regulate the supply of money in circulation.

FISCAL POLICY—The method adopted by the Government to produce and spend revenues.

FISCAL YEAR—A 12-month period, not necessarily coincidental with the calendar year, used for accounting purposes. In the case of the Federal Government, it runs from July 1 through June 30.

GALLOPING INFLATION—A rapid increase in prices without foreseeable limit.

GOLD RESERVE—The monetary stock of gold in a nation's treasury.

GOLD STANDARD—Attaching the value of a nation's currency to a fixed quantity of gold, with the currency freely exchangeable for gold at the established rate.

GROSS NATIONAL PRODUCT—A nation's total output of goods and services.

GNP DEFLATOR—The price index of all the goods and services making up the gross national product.

GUIDELINE PRINCIPAL—The voluntary limitation of wage increases in any given year to the increases in the average rate of production per man hour.

HEDGING—The technique of buying and selling which minimizes the risk of loss from price fluctuation. When used as a defense against inflation, hedging generally means buying something which may be sold at a profit, to offset the losses one incurs from steadily increasing prices.

INCOME, DISCRETIONARY—That part of an individual's income from which postponable purchases may be made —or which may be set aside as savings.

INCOME, DISPOSABLE—That part of an individual's income remaining after deductions for all types of taxes and government fees.

INCOME, NATIONAL—The sum total of wages, salaries, fringe benefits, net interest, rents, business income, profits, and income of the self-employed.

INCOME, PERSONAL—The amount of current income received by a person from all sources.

INCOME, REAL—The buying power of the income of an individual or a country.

INFLATION, CREEPING—A gradual but steady increase in the cost of goods and services.

INFLATION, COST-PUSH—A type of inflation in which rising costs push prices up.

INFLATION, DEMAND-PULL—A type of inflation in which scarcity of goods and strong demand combine to bring about a rise in prices.

INFLATION, RUNAWAY OR GALLOPING—A rapid increase in prices without foreseeable limit.

INFLATION, SUPPRESSED—A situation where inflationary pressures are contained by rationing of goods and by price controls.

INSTALLMENT CREDIT—Credit in which repayment is made at regular periods, including interest and service charges.

INSTALLMENT DEBT—The total amount owed by an individual or business which must be repaid over a specified period.

INSURANCE POLICY, FACE VALUE OF—The amount of money paid as a death benefit.

INTEREST—The cost one must pay over a period of time for the use of a sum of money.

INTEREST, PRIME RATE OF—The rate charged by banks for short-term loans to their best customers.

INVENTORY—The supply of goods a firm keeps on hand to meet needs promptly and assure an uninterrupted operation of the business.

LIABILITY—A debt or an amount of money owed by an individual or a company to others.

MARKET, BEAR—A market in which prices of most stocks are declining.

MARKET, BULL—A market in which prices of most stocks are rising.

MARKET, BUYER'S—A market in which buyers have an advantage because supply has exceeded demand and prices have come down.

MARKET, SELLER'S—A market in which supply is short and in which sellers may raise their prices and still dispose of their goods.

MONETARY POLICY—Government policy determining the amount of growth in credit and money supply.

MONEY MARKET—A term applied to the financial institutions which handle the purchase, sale and transfer of credit instruments.

MONEY SUPPLY—The total amount of money in the nation's economy, including currency (coins and dollar bills) and checking accounts.

MORTGAGE—A pledge of particular property as security for payment of a debt.

MORTGAGE MARKET—A term referring to the financial institutions which offer funds for mortgages.

MUTUAL FUND—A method of pooling your money with others' to make stock purchases through an investment company.

NATIONAL DEBT—The total indebtedness of the national government.

NATIONAL INCOME—The sum total of wages, salaries, net interest, rents, business income, profits, and income of the self-employed.

NATIONAL WEALTH—The total money value of a nation's assets at any particular time.

NET PROFITS—The amount left over after a business has paid all its bills and taxes.

NET WORTH—The excess of assets over liabilities.

PERSONAL INCOME—The amount of current income received by a person from all sources.

PREFERRED STOCK—A corporation's capital stock which has preference over common stock with respect to the payment of dividends.

PRICE CONTROL—Regulation of prices by the government to curb increase in the cost of living.

PRICE-EARNINGS RATIO—The market price of a company's stock as a multiple of the firm's net earnings per share.

PRICE FIXING—An agreement among competitors to charge identical prices and thus avoid competition.

PRIME RATE OF INTEREST—The rate charged by banks for short-term loans to their best customers.

PRINTING PRESS MONEY—Money printed by a national government to cover expenses it cannot meet through normal methods of collecting revenues.

PRODUCTIVITY—The goods and services turned out by a worker within a certain period of time.

PROFIT AND LOSS STATEMENT—A summary of revenues and expenses for a specific period.

PROFITS, GROSS—What is left after a business pays all its bills.

PROFITS, NET—The amount left over after a business has paid all its bills and taxes.

PROFIT SHARING—An extra payment to investors and employees, above their regular wages and salaries, as their participation in the profits of their company.

PROFIT SQUEEZE—A decline in profits as a per cent of sales.

PROFITEERING—The making of unreasonably large profits through the sale of goods and services.

PROMISSORY NOTE—A written promise from one person to pay another a specified sum—with interest—on a given date.

PUMP PRIMING—Expenditures by the government designed to stimulate business activity and achieve full employment.

REAL INCOME—The buying power of the income of an individual or a country.

REAL WAGE—The purchasing power of a worker's earnings.

RECESSION—A decline, across the board, in business activity, generally lasting (on the basis of post-World War II experience in the United States) about one year.

RECOVERY—A forward movement in business activity following the low point in a depression or recession.

REDEMPTION—In the economic sense, the exchange of bonds for cash.

REFLATION—A form of inflation which takes place during a period of recovery, when prices are restored to some desirable former level.

REQUIRED RESERVES—The percent of deposits that U.S. commercial banks must set aside with the Federal Reserve.

RETAILER—A merchant who sells goods to the ultimate consumer.

RUNAWAY INFLATION—A rapid increase in prices without foreseeable limit.

SALES TAX—A flat percentage tax levied on the selling price of an item.

SELLER'S MARKET—A market in which supply is short and in which sellers may raise their prices and still dispose of their goods.

SOCIAL SECURITY PROGRAM—A public welfare program designed to reduce the threat to the economic security of the individual.

SPECULATION—To assume high risks with the hope of achieving high gains.

STANDARD OF LIVING—The food, clothing, housing, medical care, goods and services which a family buys.

STOCK, BLUE CHIP—The common stock of a large corporation with a well-established record of earnings and dividends.

STOCK, COMMON—The capital stock of a corporation, giving the holder an ownership interest in the corporation's earnings and assets after prior claims have been met.

STOCK DIVIDEND—Authorized but previously unissued shares of stock in a corporation that are paid as a dividend to stockholders.

STOCK EXCHANGE—An organized marketplace in which stocks are bought and sold.

STOCK OPTION—A contract which guarantees the buyer the privilege of buying or selling a certain amount of stock at a specific price within a given period of time.

STOCK, PREFERRED—Capital stock which has preference over the common stock of a corporation with respect to the payment of dividends.

STOCK, "WATERED"—Common stock issued by a corporation which doesn't receive full payment for it.

STRATEGIC STOCKPILE—Storage by the government of certain goods deemed essential to national defense.

SUPPRESSED INFLATION—A situation where inflationary pressures are contained by rationing of goods and by price controls.

SURTAX—The application of an additional tax levy, generally a percentage, on a base tax.

TAKE-HOME PAY—The amount of money an employee actually receives in any given pay period.

TARIFF—A form of tax on the import of goods, payable when the goods cross the receiving nation's boundary.

TIGHT MONEY—A term which describes a condition of high interest rates and scarcity of credit.

TIME DEPOSIT—Money held in the bank account of an individual or a firm for which the bank requires advance notice for withdrawal.

TIME STUDY—The determination of the time required by a capable person working at a normal pace to do a specific job.

USURY—Excessively high rate of interest.

VALUE—The worth or price of goods and services.

WAGE CONTROL—National control and stabilization of wages.

WAGE, REAL—The purchasing power of a worker's earnings.

WHOLESALE PRICE INDEX—A monthly measure of changes in wholesale prices compiled by the Bureau of Labor Statistics.

WHOLESALER—One who is engaged in buying goods from producers for resale to other business firms for their own use or for final sale to consumers.

WORKING CAPITAL—The margin of current assets over current liabilities.

WORTH, NET—The excess of assets over liabilities.

Index to Charts